S0-ARN-941

We Speak as One

We Speak as One

Twelve Nobel Laureates Share Their Vision for Peace

Edited by Arthur Zajonc

www.peacejam.org

Made possible through the generous
support of the Fetzer Institute

ISBN 0-615-13323-1
©2006 PeaceJam Foundation
All Photographs by Ivan Suvanjieff
Designed by Hans Teensma
and Pamela Glaven, Impress, Inc.
Printed in the United States

Dedicated to the memory of Sir Joseph Rotblat

Introduction

Each of us witnesses injustices, small and large, nearby and far away. In the face of suffering and violence, what do we do? Do we speak out and take action, or do we remain silent and complacent? The civil rights leader Martin Luther King, Jr., wrote that "He who accepts evil without protesting against it is really cooperating with it . . . In the end, we will remember not the words of our enemies, but the silence of our friends." Like King, Archbishop Desmond Tutu pressed those sitting on the fence to take sides. In a moral issue as clear cut as apartheid in South Africa, how can anyone remain undecided and inactive? In the years before the fall of apartheid Tutu declared,

> You have no option but to be involved in the struggle and I call
> on you to be involved in the struggle for this new South Africa.
> I call on you to know that it is God's struggle. You say: But you
> will get into trouble. Of course! Who ever saw powerful people
> give up their power without doing anything? The powerful will
> get angry. So what, what is new? Tell me something else. I invite
> you to come into this exhilarating enterprise, God's enterprise,

to change this country, to transfigure this country, to make this country what it is going to become, a land where all, black, white, green, whatever, will be able to hold hands together because they are then living as those whom God has created in his image, as brothers and sisters, as members of one family. If we are the representatives of God, we must take sides. We have no choice really. To be neutral in a situation of injustice is to have chosen sides already.

The individuals we meet in these pages differ in many respects, but in this regard they are identical. None of them has stood by silently when injustice was done; rather, in the midst of tragedy they have spoken and acted regardless of the consequences. When Betty Williams heard of British soldiers firing at IRA member Danny Lennon in his speeding car, and then the horrible crash, she ran to the terrible scene of Anne Corrigan Maguire and her three small children — Joanne, John and six-week-old Andrew — dead or injured. The death of these three small children and the serious injury of their mother caused Máiread Corrigan Maguire, Ciaran McKeown, Betty Williams, and many other ordinary citizens in Northern Ireland to speak out not only against this single incident, but against all the senseless violence so common to their homeland. More than three thousand people were killed in Northern Ireland during "The Troubles" of ethnic/political conflict which lasted from the late 1960's to the 1998 Good Friday Agreement. Reflecting on the beginnings of the peace movement and the origins of Northern Ireland's Peace People, Betty Williams has said,

> We gave a voice to something that the women of Ireland were feeling at that time. They were sick of losing their husbands, sons and daughters. They were in enormous pain. I think probably when we yelled for peace — because that's what we really did, you know — the women responded in kind. The death of three children started the peace movement in Northern Ireland.

• • •

Becoming the voice for those who have died or suffered turns the light of public attention to the speaker, and as Tutu remarked, getting involved can get you into trouble. Máiread Corrigan Maguire and others in the peace movement received death threats when they cried out at the loss of loved ones. During peace marches they endured slander and pelting with bottles, sticks and stones. The methods of intimidation are always the same although they vary in brutality. In Guatemala, 400 Mayan villages were destroyed, hundreds of thousands were arrested, tortured, and imprisoned. Over 100,000 Maya Indians were killed by right-wing military death squads. Rigoberta Menchú Tum and her family continue to receive death threats to this day. Shirin Ebadi stood up for those without human rights or legal recourse in Iran. As a result, she faced long months of imprisonment herself, and her name was added to a list of death squad targets during a period of great terror and oppression in her country. In Argentina, thousands of students and liberals "disappeared" during the Dirty War of 1976 to 1983. We now know they were taken to one of 340 secret detention camps, where they were tortured and humiliated before being murdered. Adolfo Pérez Esquivel was one of those taken and tortured.

Yet in the face of it all one discovers the true greatness of the human spirit. Instead of being crushed by brutality, many individuals rise to meet the violence, demonstrating a deep faithfulness to their friends and to their cause. Even gentleness and forgiveness can appear in the ashes of destruction. We have seen the images: solo cello played amidst the ruins of Sarajevo, the reconciliation of oppressor and victim in East Timor. These are real world events that demonstrate that the human spirit can rise like a phoenix from the ashes even in the face of inconceivable cruelty.

The appalling treatment of one human by another that I have described is unlike the random violence which goes on every day in cities around the world. The central motives are not theft, sexual depravity, or drug dependence. No, the root causes are deeper: racism, sectarianism, ethnic hatred, greed, lust for power. Each of the individuals featured in this book has not only given voice to the immediate tragedy, suffering or injustice they witnessed, but they have faced the deeper causes of that tragedy and have confronted the system that relentlessly perpetrated the violence, be it a nation-state or fanatical organization. Apartheid, for example, was not comprised merely of isolated racist acts, but rather it had become a legally binding system of governance. The very institutions meant to protect the people of a country were drawn into the cycle of repression. Courts of law and police enforced unfair laws enacted by racist legislatures representing a small white minority. In order to meet such organized oppression a single individual is not sufficient. Thus, while we will meet a dozen Nobel Laureates in these pages, they are merely the most prominent representatives of a vast community who have joined with them in opposing oppression and social injustice, and advocating for the human being and for the environment. Each of them carries countless others in their hearts. When Oscar Arias accepted the Nobel Prize in 1987 he, like so many before him, remembered the thousands who had worked energetically together to end the war in Central America. He said,

> I do not receive this prize as Oscar Arias. Nor do I receive it as President of my country. I lack the arrogance to claim to represent anyone or anything, but I do not fear the humility which identifies me with the great causes shared by all. I receive it as one of four hundred million Latin Americans, who seek — in the return to freedom and in the practice of democracy — the way to overcome tremendous misery and injustice.

The forces of oppression are, therefore, met by an often invisible or underappreciated group of individuals. Each person must make the impossible decision whether or not to risk harm to themselves and to their families in order to speak and act against injustice. Wangari Maathai describes going from village to village, from family to family, speaking around the fire, especially with women, about their lives and shared suffering. Such conversation helps them make the choice that will make all the difference. In spirit they are joined with thousands of others sitting around other fires in the highlands of Kenya, all part of a single dispersed conversation. They not only share suffering, but in listening from the heart they give each other the comfort and encouragement that stems from compassion. What appears to be a mass movement of opposition is really a confederacy of thousands of individuals who ultimately make the miraculous decision to join the struggle against a cruel system of tyranny that denies them their true humanity. Adolfo Pérez Esquivel speaks of many small invisible rivers converging to form a great social movement. "I always speak of small rivers which can't be seen but unite at some great point and in some determined moment. Those rivers are small historical movements of resistance which will contribute to one great cause that has the ability to change the world."

The confluence of these tiny streams cuts across all differences. People from diverse faiths, races, and ethnicities come together in recognition of our one humanity. They seek out a harmony among the varied peoples of this small planet. As the Dalai Lama has observed,

> Looking around, I see that it is not only we Tibetan refugees, and members of other displaced communities, who face difficulties. Everywhere and in every society, people endure suffering and adversity — even those who enjoy freedom and material prosperity. Indeed, it seems to me that much of the unhappiness we humans endure is actually of our own making. In principle, therefore, this at least is avoidable. I also see that, in general, those individuals whose conduct is ethically positive are happier and more satisfied than those who neglect ethics. This confirms my belief that if we can reorient our thoughts and emotions, and reorder our behavior, not only can we learn to cope with suffering more easily, but we can prevent a great deal of it from arising in the first place.

What are the characteristics of the Dalai Lama's "positive ethics"? In the face of systemic oppression in Tibet, Latin America, and throughout the world, to what strategy do these many individuals turn? Again and again in this volume we will hear the appeal to nonviolent action. Instead of armed struggle, these voices confront violence with peaceful resistance. Gandhi's words and example have inspired millions. His advice has been a guide to them, as when he said, "wherever you are confronted with an opponent, conquer him with love. I have found that this law of love has answered as the law of destruction has never done." In the face of violence we normally react by seeking revenge, and so the cycle of violence is begun. Each act that was meant to settle a score only adds to the intensity of mutual hatred. One can break this destructive cycle only by rejecting vengeance for nonviolence and the law of love.

While completely committed to alleviating the immediate suffering of those around them, these Nobel Laureates also have sought out and spoken of the root causes of injustice and violence. In the following pages they will speak to us concerning the tragic implications of ignorance and fear in human society. The red scare fueled McCarthyism, and an analogous fear today fuels much of our reaction to terrorism. In addition to identifying the deeper causes of oppression, these men and women have attempted to live uncompromising lives committed to truth and compassion, often at great risk to themselves. Under arrest in Burma, Aung San Suu Kyi has written in her letters, "Some have questioned the appropriateness of talking about such matters as *metta* (loving-kindness) and *thissa* (truth) in the political context. But politics is about people, and what we had seen . . . proved that love and truth can move people more strongly than any form of coercion." One who embodies love and truth reaches into the hearts and minds of all those who have not lost their humanity. Even those who are the oppressors, whether soldier or terrorist, can often be touched by the power of love and truth. This is the open secret of nonviolent opposition. As Martin Luther King, Jr., put it, "At the center of nonviolence stands the principle of love."

In her reference to *metta* and *thissa*, that is, to loving-kindness and truth, Aung San Suu Kyi indirectly touches on a resource that all of the Nobels draw on. In Aung San Suu Kyi's case her arrest and solitude have become the occasion for deep and disciplined meditation based on the Buddhist teachings of her Burmese monks. But she is not alone. The Dalai Lama leads his own lonely struggle on a very public stage. In their own way, each of the Nobels has found a means of drawing on the invisible spiritual resources available to everyone. In times of exhaustion, doubt, tragedy or pain, each has discovered the undeniable capacity available to all that allows us to retain our humanity in every circumstance.

Finally, these Nobels are committed to the future, and they express this by working tirelessly with youth. Since 1996, Nobel Peace Prize winners have been working directly with youth as part of PeaceJam's unique program of education and youth activism. Every year all over the world thousands of high school–aged youth come together with one of the Nobels featured here (to date, 120 of these PeaceJam Youth Conferences have been held). These young people represent thousands of others who have been study-ing part of the PeaceJam curriculum in their schools. Through that wide-ranging curriculum students learn not only about the Nobel Laureate they will meet, but also they study important themes selected by the Nobel Laureates themselves.

Based on her experience in creating the International Campaign to Ban Landmines, Jody Williams teaches young people that "Individuals Can Make a Difference." Rigoberta Menchú Tum has chosen to work with them on "Healing Communities Torn by Racism and Violence," a theme arising from her work with oppressed indigenous communities in Guatemala. Máiread Corrigan Maguire tackles the problem of "Building a New Culture of Nonviolence for the Human Family," and Betty Williams helps young people find "Community-based Solutions to the Problem of Violence." Adolfo Pérez Esquivel of Argentina wrestles with the issue of "Human Rights and Justice for All." Based on his work in East Timor, José Ramos-Horta has chosen to work with teens on "Creating Peace and Democracy," and because of his work with the Truth and Reconciliation Commission in South Africa, Desmond Tutu teaches young people about "Making Friends out of Enemies," while Costa Rica's famous President Oscar Arias instructs students concerning "Guns,

Violence, and the International Arms Trade." The exile leader of Tibet, the Dalai Lama addresses "Ecology and the Human Heart," and nuclear physicist Joseph Rotblat explored strategies for "Creating a Safer World" with his protégés. Shirin Ebadi works with young people about "Defending the Rights of Women and Children," and Wangari Maathai has taught young PeaceJammers to take up "Protecting the Environment and Creating a Culture of Peace." Finally, Aung San Suu Kyi, who has been under house arrest all these ten years, has been held as a great heroine and example to many thousands of PeaceJam participants. Even in her absence, her curriculum has helped many who are committed to "Building Democratic Societies." Through PeaceJam our world's most potent advocates for peace have agreed to share their insights and passion with hundreds of thousands of young people because they know that the future will lie in their hands and be shaped by what lives in their hearts. PeaceJam gatherings marry the idealism of youth with the mature commitments of the Peace Laureates whose lives have been unswervingly dedicated to stopping senseless violence against our fellow human beings.

When Jody Williams meets with young people, they discover the power of commitment and individual action:

> For me, the most important thing is finding a way to put what you believe into concrete action. Words are lovely. I like words. But when I'm talking about the issues that confront us, words aren't enough. Words without action to back them up consistently are irrelevant. And any of us can take steps to begin to find ways to bring about change. Anybody can do it. If I did it — anybody can do it. And if you are not going to do it yourself, step aside and let those of us who are committed have more room to move.

One of the best strategies to insure peace is to educate a new generation of peacemakers. In 1994 the seeds for PeaceJam sprouted in Denver with Dawn Gifford Engle and Ivan Suvanjieff, and in my own heart at my first meeting with the Dalai Lama. Unbeknownst to me, Dawn and Ivan had developed the vision for PeaceJam, and had invited the Dalai Lama and many other Nobel Peace Laureates to work with young people in a sustained and powerful way. Meanwhile, I was granted the honor of attending a series of small meetings with the Dalai Lama at Columbia University, and my fourteen-year-old son Tristan was allowed to help set up chairs and be present as well. Over meals I would talk with Tristan about the sessions, and invariably his views of them were insightful and his suggestions for themes and questions were often better than those of the contributing academics. In that moment I felt the potential importance of bringing young people together with the Dalai Lama, but I had no way to actualize this vision until I met Dawn Gifford Engle. I shared my enthusiasm and ideas for working with the Dalai Lama, and learned that she and Ivan had already gotten agreement from him and six other Nobel Laureates to work with youth. As luck would have it I was about to begin a two-year term as Program Director at the Fetzer Institute, a Michigan foundation. I suggested that we propose the PeaceJam Program to the leadership and board of the Fetzer Institute. Since then the Fetzer Institute has been a crucial sponsor of PeaceJam, funding especially its curriculum design and supporting PeaceJam's early development. I believe that Dawn, Ivan and I were all listening to the voice of youth and so came to a common vision, although we were thousands of miles apart. But we needed to find each other and work together in order to make that vision a reality. It has been a privilege to work with Dawn and Ivan. My contributions have been modest in comparison to theirs, but as I witness the tremendous growth of PeaceJam, and the heart-warming work of young people all over the world, I am deeply encouraged.

From 1996 to 2006 PeaceJam events have taken place serving over 500,000 young people either directly through weekend gatherings with one of the Peace Prize winners, or through studying the curriculum and performing the volunteer activities that bring PeaceJam alive in their schools around the world. In September 2006 for the first time, nearly all of the PeaceJam Nobel Laureates will gather in Denver. They will meet with each other and with 3,000 young people in order to celebrate ten years of PeaceJam work, and to rededicate their efforts for the years ahead. In preparation for this event, PeaceJam founders Dawn Gifford Engle and Ivan Suvanjieff traveled the globe interviewing all of PeaceJam's Nobelists. By doing so they brought them into a global dialogue that will continue in Denver and the coming years, and I am using these new interviews to further this global conversation. In these pages I want to bring each of these remarkable women and men closer to you, and by weaving their diverse thoughts together, also bring them closer to each other. While each of them is a giant in their own right, we never see so many Nobel Peace Laureates together and in deep conversation. The gathering of Nobel Peace Laureates in Denver will be the largest ever held in U.S. history. By bringing them into relationship with each other, both in these pages and in Denver, we hope that the coherence of their essential message becomes clear and that the power of their work continues to grow to become far greater than the sum of its parts.

When asked about the future PeaceJam event planned for September of 2006, Nobel Peace Laureate Jose Ramos-Horta responded,

> What is most interesting for me is the encounter with thousands of youth from different ethnic, cultural and social backgrounds, coming together with one goal, and that is to promote human solidarity, understanding, tolerance and peace. We should not underestimate the tremendous energy and power of the youth. Together with the Nobel Peace Laureates, they can do enormous good to help the neediest people of the world.

By holding the suffering of the neediest before us, we are called to move beyond words and hopes to actions. Jose Ramos-Horta's message to his fellow Nobel Peace Prize winners is simultaneously a message to us all. What might we do together as a confederacy of compassionate individuals committed to direct action in support of those who need it most?

• • •

The silence of the good was remarked on by Edmund Burke in his justly famous line, "All that is required for evil to prevail is for good men to do nothing." During his time in prison Adolfo Pérez Esquivel had time to ponder the words of Burke and King. Later he would write, "Martin Luther King's idea certainly applies here, because the evils in Latin America, as in so many other places, are the result of the silence of the good, the silence of those who don't get really and deeply involved with their brothers and sisters. I've thought a lot about this—the silence of the good. Involvement always costs. It's not hard to understand why we have been the victims of repression and persecution." Perhaps this is the most important message these men and women can offer us: get involved! It is a message they have lived, and they invite us to join them in that common work of acting on behalf of humanity and the Earth. As the co-founder of PeaceJam Dawn Gifford Engle says, "There are more than two billion teenagers on this planet. Nearly half of the world's population is under the age of 20. The message that PeaceJam and the Nobel Laureates have for young people around the world is that, yes, one person really can make a difference." And we are all called to action by the shining example of these Nobel Laureates of courage and peace.

—ARTHUR ZAJONC

Part One

The Laureates

In these pages we will meet twelve Nobel Peace Laureates who have worked with the youth of PeaceJam, and we memorialize a thirteenth who has recently died. Each has spent their adult life in service to others and to a vision of a just and compassionate society. Individually and collectively they exemplify the promise of humanity. Before I convene the conversation between them all, we must encounter and appreciate their individual contributions to the betterment of our world. We need to meet them first as idealistic young men and women who confronted extraordinary life circumstances with courage, compassion and growing intelligence, and who have matured into lifelong leaders in the global movement for peace and environmental action. Each offers us a view into the mysterious and completely particular destiny of the individual. Yet for all the differences between them and their specific tasks, we can sense a profound commonality which I take to be the moral foundation that guides their relentless striving for the good. They have all witnessed social injustice, cruelty, and the abuse of power. And they have all answered these dark dimensions of human society with heartfelt concern, with the light of moral insight, and above all with decisive nonviolent action.

— A.Z.

1

Desmond Tutu

Truth, Reconciliation and Forgiveness

By his own recollection in his book *No Future Without Forgiveness*, the most important event in the childhood of Desmond Tutu concerned a simple gesture of respect shown to his mother. In an interview with PeaceJam he recalled,

> I know that I owe a very, very great deal to other people, and one of the people who influenced me most of all was Trevor Huddleston. I was standing with my mother — as I said, my mother was a domestic worker, she was a cook at an institution for blind women — we were standing outside the hostel and a white man walked past; he was in a long white cassock with a huge sombrero, and as he stepped past us (I must've been about 9 or so), he doffed his hat to my mother. At the time when it happened, I wasn't aware that it was something that would become so indelible in my life. I was seeing a white man doffing his hat for a black woman? An uneducated woman? Later when I went to theological college, I realized that this man was living

out what he believed about us, that each one of us is created in
the image of God, and that you have this incredible dignity and
worth and that really, we all belong.

In a simple act of respect toward a woman of another race, the young
Desmond Tutu perceived an entire worldview, one in which every human
being was of equal value, one in which we all possess inherent dignity.
These are views Tutu also has lived out in his own life in South Africa.

Archbishop Desmond Tutu was born in 1931 in a gold mining town west
of Johannesburg called Klerksdorp. He grew up within a culture of discrim-
ination where the dominant minority white population routinely treated
the majority black African population as inferior, indeed as a lesser
species. Apartheid had been introduced in 1948 by the Nationalist Party as

a means of maintaining white control over a black population five times its size. Blacks were segregated into "homelands," and were severely restricted in their movement and ability to associate in groups. They were subject to arrest and detention without a proper trial, and had to carry a "pass" with them at all times specifying their homeland and travel restrictions. In countless ways, black South Africans were treated with disrespect, so it is not surprising that a gesture of respect would stand out in the memory of Desmond Tutu when he was a young boy.

Trevor Huddleston became a guiding figure and formative force for the young Tutu. When Tutu was hospitalized for a year and a half in his late teens, the Anglican priest Huddleston visited him in the hospital. Lack of funds kept Tutu from studying to be a physician, and turned him towards the profession of schoolteacher like his father. After three years of struggle teaching within the Bantu educational system restricted to blacks, Tutu resigned his post and turned instead to the same profession as his mentor Huddleston.

After completing seminary and a period in London, Desmond Tutu returned to South Africa and in 1975 was the first black to be appointed Dean of St. Mary's Cathedral. He went on to serve as Bishop of Lesotho and in 1978 was made General Secretary of the South African Council of Churches. From these positions of distinction within the Anglican Church, Archbishop Tutu led the church's opposition to the pernicious policies of apartheid and segregation. Tutu spoke out forcefully against all of the government policies designed to subjugate the black population, refusing to carry the pass. Whether at home or abroad, Tutu was a relentless advocate for the overthrow of apartheid by all peaceful, nonviolent means. For his leadership in the struggle Desmond Tutu was awarded the 1984 Nobel Peace Prize. Since then he has labored tirelessly for his people and the peoples of the world.

When, after 28 years, Nelson Mandela was released from prison in 1990, the long-held vision became reality and apartheid fell. Nelson Mandela and Desmond Tutu then took up the common work of recreating a new South Africa. While Mandela reformed the government, Tutu headed an entirely new kind of judicial body designed to memorialize the suffering of black South Africans at the hands of their white countrymen, but simultaneously to allow for reconciliation and even forgiveness through the workings of a Truth and Reconciliation Commission. Tutu illustrates the power of forgiveness by sharing his experiences:

> I was sitting in my office minding my own business when a young man came in who had been tortured in detention, and I still remember so vividly him saying to me, "You know, Father, when these people are torturing you, and they say that we are in charge, you say 'Yes, they are running this country.' But you look at them and you see these are God's children and they are losing their humanity. They need us to help them recover that humanity." And I remember a white woman who had survived a hand grenade attack, but it had left her so badly injured that she spent six months in ICU, and when she was discharged she could not do things for herself — she had to be helped by her children to bathe, to clothe, to eat. She said of the experience that it had enriched her life, and she said, "I want to meet the person who did this in a spirit of forgiveness; I want to forgive him," and she went on to say, "and I hope he will forgive me."

Against this background of his long struggles in South Africa, we asked Desmond Tutu as he looked into the future, what were his greatest hopes and fears for humanity.

> I, myself, have very great hope for the world. We face enormous problems — there is hunger, there's conflict, there is poverty; we particularly in Southern Africa are being devastated by the HIV/AIDS pandemic, and in a way, you almost want to say there is no hope, the world is going down the tubes. But I think, "No!" There are these fantastic people, the young peo-

ple, especially, who dream dreams, and I think that is one of our greatest hopes — young people who are idealistic, who really do believe that the world can become a better place. So it is young people — not exclusively — but it is largely young people who have usually demonstrated against war, who have demonstrated against international institutions that seem to favor the affluent, and they are saying, "This world can become a better place. This world can become a place that is hospitable to peace, to justice, to compassion." And so, I dream that one day we will help to actualize, to bring to reality, the dream that young people have, which is God's dream, that we will come to realize that we are family, we belong together. And what would therefore be the thing that I fear most? What I fear most is that we will not discover the truth about ourselves. We will constantly think that it is possible to go it alone — we will constantly be wanting to be selfish. We will want to spend obscene amounts on instruments of death and destruction when we know we could use only a very small fraction of that to enable all of God's children everywhere to have clean water, to have enough to eat, lovely schools and homes, yes. And I just hope, I mean, that young people will say, "Oldies, just get out of the way."

At the thought of oldies, like himself, getting pushed out of the way, Tutu gave a great laugh, his eyes sparkling with mischief. His own laughter is not unlike that of one of his fellow Nobel Peace Laureates, the Dalai Lama. When we asked Tutu whether he had any questions for the other Nobel Laureates who are part of PeaceJam, the playful glint returned to his eyes and he responded, "The other Nobel Laureates? I would like to ask my friend the Dalai Lama, how does he retain his serenity? And how does he manage to be so mischievous?"

In this moment we experience one individual, a black man from South Africa, thinking with delight of a friend far away, a Tibetan in exile. Both have suffered personally and witnessed even greater suffering. They have felt the pain of millions, and yet neither has ceased celebrating life or lost their sense of humor. Later when interviewing the Dalai Lama we did ask him Tutu's question. The Dalai Lama laughed heartily at the question, replying, "I think that the serenity belongs to me; the mischievousness belongs to some of my friends, including Archbishop Tutu." He laughed again with a laugh known around the world, and then explained something about their special relationship. "Because to play means you need someone to play with. So whenever we see each other and I see his face, his eyes, I want to say something, and he equally responds to me, very mischievous. I love it!" And again he gave in fully to laughter at the thought of his distant mischievous companion and fellow champion for peace. The relationship between Desmond Tutu and the Dalai Lama can stand for us as an emblem or symbol for the weaving together of voices, deeds, and affections that seek to heal and lift up all parts of our world.

2

Jody Williams
Individuals Make a Difference

The country might be Afghanistan or Angola or Mozambique. The setting is a rural countryside where a group of children are kicking a ball or can among themselves. An especially swift kick sends the object flying into the brush at the side of the clearing where the children play. Reflexively, one of the children runs laughing after the errant ball. Perhaps a mother notices and calls out to stop him, but before he can turn to hear her an explosion rips through the air and through his body. Another precious child has been maimed or killed by a long-forgotten landmine.

Events such as these occur every day. An average of 500 victims are injured or killed each week due to unexploded landmines and ordnance left behind after war, which translates into 26,000 injured each year. In a 1994 report, the United Nations estimated 250,000 injuries or deaths had been caused by landmines. That number has probably climbed to over 500,000 in the last ten years. Since World War II, 400 million landmines have been deployed and over 80 million in the last 25 years alone. Countries like Afghanistan, Angola, Cambodia, Mozambique, Croatia, and Bosnia-

Herzegovina are the most severely mined countries in the world, an inheritance left over from a violent past. Unlike the soldiers who planted these weapons, landmines never return home. They remain behind, ready to kill. Jody Williams, founding-coordinator of the International Campaign to Ban Landmines (ICBL), and co-author of *After the Guns Fall Silent*, has put is this way.

> Landmines distinguish themselves because once they have been sown, once the soldier walks away from the weapon, the landmine cannot tell the difference between a soldier or a civilian — a woman, a child, a grandmother going out to collect firewood to make a family meal . . . The landmine is eternally prepared to take victims . . . It is the perfect soldier, the "eternal sentry."

. . .

Jody Williams and the ICBL have worked tenaciously to ban landmines throughout the world. For their remarkable efforts they were awarded the 1997 Nobel Peace Prize.

Jody Williams was born in Putney, Vermont, in 1950. After completing a Master's in International Relations from Johns Hopkins in 1984, Jody Williams coordinated the Nicaragua-Honduras Education Project. Following this she developed and directed humanitarian relief projects in El Salvador. While working in Central America, Williams grew to appreciate the efforts of aid workers, many of them in the Catholic Church, who tried desperately to give spiritual and material comfort to the poor and oppressed. She had grown up Catholic, but for the first time saw the inspiring sight of priests, nuns and laity "walking with the poor." Some of them were slain by military death squads along with the peasants they served, martyred not because they sought death but because they sought to do good. She learned that "When the killers kill, they expect to make everyone else too afraid to do anything. But that is not what happened in El Salvador." The death of a friend would inspire others to step forward to continue to walk with the poor, in memory of the person who had died caring for others. The chain of service and sacrifice was only strengthened by the senseless carnage of oppression and death.

Growing up with her deaf and schizophrenic brother, Stephen, Jody Williams felt specially prepared for her difficult and often heart-wrenching work with the wounded poor during the civil war that raged in El Salvador from 1980 to 1992. She and her whole family had been challenged to their limits by her brother's violent behavior, but in the end Jody was grateful for what it gave her as inner resources on which she could draw in tough times. The challenge of life with Stephen had strengthened her for work with children of war, some of whom she brought back to the U.S. for crucial medical attention. Later she wrote about her feelings to her parents, thanking them and her brother.

. . .

But if it were not for Stephen, if he had not been my brother and affected me the way that he did, these children [from El Salvador] would be deaf or dead or god knows what. So, his pain and suffering has brought joy and life where it otherwise might not have been. So I guess I am trying to say to you, thank you for the gift of Stephen — all the joy and sorrow and everything that knowing him has been and will continue to be. But because of him, the lives of others who don't even know him have been changed — for the better — forever.

Everything is interconnected. The capacities Jody Williams was able to bring to her work were schooled through her prior life. It had been hard growing up loving and caring for a disabled brother, but exactly this challenge had shaped her, made her stronger and more compassionate than she would have been otherwise. In a strange and remarkable way, Stephen's illness, refined by Jody's love, aided dozens of children in distant El Salvador. Such is Jody Williams' vision of the world.

Equally important to Jody Williams is the conviction that everyone can act to oppose injustice or relieve suffering. In her conversations with teenagers she tries to get them to think beyond their next visit to the mall, and instead she asks them to think about world issues, about what should be different and how they might help. She asks them:

What do you care about beyond going to the mall and buying the latest sneakers or skirt or whatever? What do you worry about in the world? And if you worry about it, why do you worry about it? And, if you're going to worry, what do you think you can do to make it different? Start thinking about it now, don't wait until you're older. Anybody can take action.

One of my favorite groups on the landmine campaign was a fourth-grade group from Morgantown, West Virginia, that saw a little piece on landmines and how it affected kids all over the world. And these fourth-graders created "Students Against Land-mines." Fourth-graders went to the university in Morgantown and did bake sales and leafleting to educate college students about the problem. If fourth-graders in Morgantown, West Virginia, can take action, anybody can take action.

Jody Williams feels it is important to direct children's attention away from TV ads and shopping to the real issues of our time. Once they attend to real-world issues, compassion is awakened and they naturally want to help. Action is available to everyone, and words alone are of little consequence. "As I said before, when talking about the issues that confront us, words aren't enough. That is what I try to make kids understand."

When PeaceJam asked Jody Williams about her greatest hopes and fears for the future she spoke about what true global security actually means. "I think, for me, the biggest challenge in the next 10-year period would be to get young people **and** old people to really think about what security means, and that's a hard one." She fears that people too quickly give over the responsibility for security to the government. "They want to believe that somebody else is going to protect them." She feels strongly that we need to look beyond our own personal and national interests to the security of the globe. Instead we spend too much time:

> making sure that no other country can threaten [our super-power] status, and that means militarily, economically, cultur-ally — in all ways. If that is your framework, you're not going to be thinking about multi-lateralism; you're not really going to be caring about what happens to the rest of the planet except in the context of how it affects your ability to use the resources of the world or your ability to project power.

She argues that true security is only possible when we break out of such self-ish, nationalistic tunnel-vision and begin to think of others, of their security, and the well-being of all. Only in this way can collaboration among all nations and peoples come about that will guarantee genuine security:

> I spoke at the U.N. in July of 2005 at a global conference on the
> role of civil society in conflict prevention, and what amazes me
> is how few people seem to make the links: that working to pro-
> tect our environment is contributing to human security; work-
> ing on disarmament is contributing to human security; work-
> ing on poverty reduction is human security. I think that we all
> need to at least say that one line: "When I fight for human
> rights, I'm fighting for a new vision of human security." "When
> I protect our environment, I'm fighting for a new vision of
> human security." "When I seek to reduce the poverty in the
> world, I'm fighting for a new vision of human security."

While Jody Williams recognizes the huge challenge this view entails, she
also possesses an unwavering confidence in the power of committed people to change the status quo. After all, starting from scratch and with few
funds, she and her colleagues in the ICBL have grown their network to
include over 1,400 non-governmental organizations, and they have gotten
154 countries to join the 1997 "Convention on the Prohibition of the Use,
Stockpiling, Production and Transfer of Anti-Personnel Mines and on
their Destruction." Her greatest hope for the future is the power of even a
few dedicated people to change everything:

> When I look into the future, my greatest hope is that enough
> people will realize that if we work together to make the world
> a better place, we actually can succeed. A handful of truly com-
> mitted people can continue to change the world. It has hap-
> pened so many times. I think if there are enough people who
> see things differently and are willing to take action, then there
> is hope. My greatest fear is worrying that not enough people
> will come together to believe that we actually can make the
> world a better place for everybody.

3

The Dalai Lama
Freedom in Exile

Writing of his own childhood in his book *Freedom in Exile*, the Dalai Lama describes the poor village of Takster in the Tibetan province of Amdo where he spent the first years of life from his birth on July 6, 1935. "Its pastures had not been settled or farmed for long, only grazed by nomads. The reason for this was the unpredictability of the weather in that area. During my early childhood, my family was one of twenty or so making a precarious living from the land there." He was born with the family name Lhamo Thondup (meaning wish-fulfilling goddess). "Of course, no one had any idea that I might be anything other than an ordinary baby. I myself likewise had no particular intimation of what lay ahead. My earliest memories are very ordinary. One thing that I remember enjoying particularly as a very young boy was going into the hen coop to collect the eggs with my mother and then staying behind. I liked to sit in the hen's nest and make clucking noises. Another favorite occupation of mine as an infant was to pack things in a bag as if I was about to go on a long journey. 'I'm going to Lhasa, I'm going to Lhasa,' I would say. This, coupled with my insistence that I be allowed always to sit at the head of

the table, was later said to be an indication that I must have known that I was destined for greater things."

Following the death of the thirteenth Dalai Lama a search process was initiated to find his reincarnation. Having been led to the modest house of Lhamo Thondup by visions and signs, the search party from Lhasa tested the three-year-old Lhamo by setting out an array of toys and treasures, only some of which had belonged to the thirteenth Dalai Lama. Without hesitation the young boy identified all the objects of the previous Dalai Lama, declaring, "It's mine. It's mine." Not long afterward the delegation was satisfied that they had indeed found the reincarnation of the thirteenth Dalai Lama, whom they also considered to be a manifestation of Avalokiteshvara, or Chenrezig, Bodhisattva of Compassion, holder of the White Lotus. The child and his family did indeed pack their bags, and they all made the long three-month trek to Lhasa where a new life of monastic education and governmental responsibilities awaited Lhamo Thondup in his new life as the Dalai Lama, the religious and secular leader of Tibet.

As a child of five, Lhamo Thondup was taken to the hilltop Potala Palace in Lhasa where he was officially installed as spiritual leader of Tibet. Soon afterwards, the newly recognized Dalai Lama was taken to Jokhang temple where he was inducted as a novice monk in a ceremony known as the "cutting of the hair." "From now on, I was to be shaven-headed and attired in maroon monk's robes," the Dalai Lama would later recall. The monastic education he received was that given to all monks. He would ultimately attain the highest level of monastic educational accomplishment, the *geshe* degree, equivalent to a doctorate in Buddhist studies.

By the time the Dalai Lama turned fifteen, relations with neighboring China had grown extremely tense and in October of 1950, 80,000 soldiers of the People's Liberation Army crossed over from China into the northeastern province of Amdo, the Dalai Lama's childhood homeland, and over the Drichu River. The plight of Tibet was dire and the Dalai Lama was therefore quickly granted the formal temporal powers that would normally have been given him somewhat later. Not long after this his eldest brother arrived in Lhasa. "As soon as I set eyes on him, I knew that he had suffered greatly. Because Amdo, the province where we were both born, and in which Kumbum is situated, lies so close to China, it had quickly fallen under control of the Communists."

At fifteen years of age the Dalai Lama found himself as the spiritual and temporal leader of six million Tibetans with the Chinese army already on Lhasa's doorstep and the threat of full-scale war hanging heavy in the high mountain air. During the next few years of violence and occupation, numerous delegations and negotiations with the Chinese were undertaken, and in 1954 the 19-year-old Dalai Lama risked capture by journeying to Peking under Chinese military escort. It is extraordinary to imagine the

Dalai Lama seated with Chairman Mao Tse-tung discussing economics, politics and governance issues. The young Dalai Lama was interested in and open to the modernization of Tibet, but concerning the core issue of spirituality they differed completely. The Dalai Lama reported that during their last meeting, after discussing conventional matters of state, "he [Mao] drew closer to me and said, 'Your attitude is good, you know. Religion is poison.' At this I felt a violent burning sensation all over my face and I was suddenly very afraid. 'So,' I thought, 'you are the destroyer of the *Dharma* after all.'". . .

In the years that followed, Tibetan armed resistance to the occupying Chinese grew. Destruction, torture and death mounted on all sides. The situation in Tibet so deteriorated that ultimately the Dalai Lama had to flee Lhasa. Dressed as a soldier, with a rifle over his shoulder and an old *thangka* painting rolled up under his arm, on March 17, 1959, he began the dangerous month-long journey over the Himalayas to India where he would ultimately set up his headquarters in exile in Dharamsala. From exile the Dalai Lama has continued to advocate for the rights of his beloved Tibetan people and homeland, always seeking nonviolent means of providing greater autonomy and religious freedom for Tibet. In 1989 his faithful efforts were recognized with the award of the Nobel Peace Prize.

During a recent visit to Arizona, PeaceJam asked the Dalai Lama about his hopes and fears for the future, just as we had asked Desmond Tutu. He responded,

> Of course, there are many kinds of challenges. But the most important one, I feel, is population. And then, also, I think, the energy crisis and the water crisis. I think these are the most important. We're not seeing the complete picture, or the holistic picture, and we're not thinking about the long-term future. This is my fear. We need a way to educate not only in one particular field, but we should also have a broader, holistic, long-term view.

· · ·

And concerning what he sees as hopeful he responded,

> Oh, we have great intelligence, and also, I think we have potential for possibly creating a sense of community that builds self-confidence, with determination and will power. So therefore, I feel basically, we do have the ability to overcome or to address these challenges.
>
> Judging from the events in the 20th Century, I am hopeful. I think humanity is becoming more mature through crisis. And unfortunately, in the 20th Century, there were a lot of crises, including wars with millions and millions of people killed and immense destruction. But the countries which suffered most, like Germany or Japan or others, they have not lost their hope. They kept their will and their hope. They were in ashes, but they rebuilt their nation and their homes, their community. Meanwhile, I think the people who witnessed this, that brand of tragedy, I think they're really dedicated to peace. And they'll not want that kind of destruction. Now, I think the younger generation, they should learn from that and think about responding to our problems not just through our emotions, but acting with a more holistic view, without losing our own hope, our own determination. Then we can work on our problems. Of course, for the world to have 100% peace, that is, of course, impossible — there are always some sorts of problems.

We also asked the Dalai Lama if he had any questions he wanted to ask any of the other Nobel Laureates who would be present at the 2006 PeaceJam event. The Dalai Lama responded with a powerful vision for the common work of the Nobel Laureates.

> One thing — ever since the Iraq crisis happened, I have very strongly felt that those individuals who can represent no one

— no country — but can be a representative of peace, a representative of humanity, including many Nobel Laureates; they should take a more active role for peace. And therefore, whenever some crisis is about to rise up, about to come, I urgently appeal to Nobel Laureates in such cases that we should come as a group, go there and talk to the key people. I feel that before the Iraq crisis, if some Nobel Laureates went to Baghdad and gave Saddam Hussein very frankly all the possibilities and consequences, I think that he as a human being and from his own selfish viewpoint, of course, he'd have to think. Even if the mission failed, nothing would be lost. This is my appeal. I wrote about this idea to President Havel and also Nelson Mandela and some others, and eventually I also personally met with them and discussed this, and Nelson Mandela was very, very supportive and President Havel was very supportive. So, I am hopeful. I am looking forward to some active role by those Nobel Peace Laureates in PeaceJam.

The Dalai Lama hopes that a group of Nobel Laureates will act collectively as humanity's representatives for peace. Perhaps by coming together with PeaceJam youth now, these Laureates are taking a first step in realizing his powerful vision of a single voice calling out and acting for peace in a way that transcends the interests of individual nation-states, races and religions.

4

Shirin Ebadi
Climbing Sheer Walls

In her new book, *Iran Awakening,* Shirin Ebadi recounts a harrowing experience. It occurred in the late nineties, when dozens of Iranian intellectuals had been murdered and the government had admitted partial complicity in their deaths. As attorney for the family of two of the victims, Shirin Ebadi was permitted a brief ten days to study the entire dossier of the judiciary's investigation. Over many pages, she read about brutal slayings and the plans for more. Strangulations, stabbings, and shootings were described as acts all done in the name of God. Late on her first day of reading she came to the transcript of a conversation between a death squad member and a government investigator. The passage she read next, the words of an assassin, haunted her for years. "The next person to be killed is Shirin Ebadi." The minister of intelligence had replied to the assassin's declaration, "Not during Ramadan, but anytime thereafter." Here she sat, seeking justice for the death of fellow Iranians who had been slain following the utterance of those same words, but without Ramadan to protect them.

• • •

The first woman to sit as a judge in Iran, and a courageous defender of the rights of activists, children, women and journalists, Shirin Ebadi was awarded the Nobel Peace Prize in 2003. The inner call to act against injustice came very early for Shirin Ebadi. In a recent interview with PeaceJam she described it in these words.

Everyone is born with certain particularities. People are not alike. None of your five fingers are the same size. From childhood, I fell in love with a phenomenon I later learned was justice. When I was a child and saw other children fighting I would go aid the underdog, without even knowing what they were fighting about, which would also cause me to get in the middle and get beaten. That is why I later became a student of law. And later, because of this feeling, I became a judge, as I thought I could help execute and bring about justice. When the Islamic Revolution came about and said a woman could no longer be a judge, I changed my job, and became a lawyer. It was the same feeling that encouraged me to become active in defending human rights. Everyone is born with a certain feeling. I believe the most fortunate of all people are the ones that go after their instincts and their nature.

Born into a family of academics and practicing Muslims in 1947, Shirin Ebadi spent her childhood "in a family filled with kindness and affection." In an interview with her in New York in 2005, PeaceJam asked Shirin Ebadi about her childhood and about the place of role models in her life. Dr. Ebadi gave us a candid view of her early years.

When I was a child, I was very devilish. My mother used to say I "climbed the sheer wall," as they say in my country. Three times I cracked my head open. My mother used to say, she never remembered a time when some part of my body was not injured as I was very much a tomboy. But this naughty child also had her wishes and dreams. Let me confess to you, from childhood I had big dreams. I always believed I would become a great person, but these great dreams had different interpretations in different times of my life. When I was a kid I wanted to become a math teacher and that was the most important person for me at that time in the world. And now I wish to help all the children in the world. As one grows up, one's own dreams also become larger.

Never in my life have I believed in role models or patterns to follow. One must live according to his or her condition and situation. I tell my daughters, don't follow me as a role model! I have had my own special situation and condition in life; your conditions and your times are different. I did not pattern my life after anyone and I hope I am not a role model for anyone. Everyone must choose his/her own path according to his/her own possibilities and condition.

• • •

Shirin Ebadi certainly followed her own good advice and forged her own way in a culture that gave little support to the professional development of women. When Iran was under the Shah, Ebadi studied law from 1965 to 1968 and immediately took the exams to become a judge. By 1975 she had risen to become president of the City Court in Tehran. Her situation changed dramatically in 1979 with the Islamic Revolution in Iran. The Islamic view held that women could not be judges, and so Ebadi and other women judges were assigned to be legal clerks in the very courts over which they had presided. Her situation became increasingly difficult, and Ebadi was even denied the right to become a practicing lawyer until 1992. From that day until the present Shirin Ebadi has consistently represented those most forgotten or oppressed in Iran: murdered students, abused children, slain journalists and women. She has done this without regard for her own safety saying, "Any person who pursues human rights in Iran must live with fear from birth to death, but I have learned to overcome my fear." Unless one can reach such equanimity in the face of real or imagined danger, one is open to manipulation. In a Tufts University lecture she pointed to anthrax letters and media distortion as generating a fear among many Americans that prepared the way for war in Iraq. Intimidation never kept Ebadi from doing what she felt was right.

The event that changed her life and put her on the course of representing murdered activists and journalists took place during the fall of 1988. Ebadi's mother-in-law received a call one cold morning from an official at Evin Prison. Seven years earlier, Shirin Ebadi's brother-in-law Faud had been sentenced to twenty years in prison for selling underground newspapers and reading idealistic socialist literature. Now the sad day arrived when the execution of this young man, without cause, was brusquely announced. Every judicial fiber of Ebadi protested. The taking of a human life was the last and most extreme judicial measure requiring exhaustive legal examination, but Faud's "trial" had lasted but a few minutes and the accusations against him were impossible fabrications. Of the night she learned of Faud's execution, Ebadi writes, "a mute fury settled in my stomach. When I think back and try to pinpoint the moment that changed me, the moment when my life took a different course, I see that it all began that night." Injustice of the gravest kind had struck her family. Many other families were also losing loved ones, and she had to do something. So she chose to help the defenseless. Again and again Shirin Ebadi would take on cases in which human rights and the rights of women and children were at stake.

In the year 2000, many legal cases later and twelve years after the execution of Faud in Evin Prison, Shirin Ebadi was arrested and taken to Evin Prison herself. She had been actively investigating the slaying of a student and poet, Ezzat, who had been sprayed with bullets by paramilitary thugs for protesting a newspaper closing. Ebadi had taken on the case without fees and in the course of her investigations an unexpected and amazing development occurred. One of the paramilitary death squad's own members became a witness on her behalf. His videotaped deposition detailed the manner and means of the murder, but when Shirin Ebadi deposited the video at the ministry, she was taken into custody, spending a month in Evin and other prisons enduring daily interrogation, until her case was ultimately dismissed. Ezzat's murder was also dismissed as well, but not before the Iranian people had learned the ugly circumstances of the murder.

Shirin Ebadi likewise "climbed sheer walls" in order to seek justice for children. When in a PeaceJam interview we quoted to her the line from Pablo Neruda, "The blood of children in the streets is like the blood of children in the streets," this was her passionate reply:

> Unfortunately, we see in most of the countries of the world, the budget for military is larger than the budget for children. This means the ignoring of children. The killing of children is not from a bullet that we fire at them but rather when we forget their rights.

We also asked Shirin Ebadi about her greatest hopes and fears for humanity in the coming years. Her thoughts immediately turned to young people and to the potential of PeaceJam's work.

· · ·

When I look into the future, my hope is the younger generation — the generations that must take the world from us and I hope pass it on to the future generation in better condition than received. As for my fear, my fear is that material things and attention to the appearance of things in life have distracted the attention of the youth from important things. I am amazed when I see some of the youth so captivated with designer clothing or the models of cars or appearance of things. It looks to me like the luxuries of life are imposing themselves over moral values. That is why I see such gatherings as PeaceJam's activities as necessary for youth. We must acquaint the youth to the realities of the world — even if these realities are not pretty. We must tell them how many children are deprived of schooling. We must tell them that millions of people in the world have no access to drinking water. We must tell them what war means and how far into the future the damages of war will affect us. The younger generation must know how many schools could be built with the cost of producing just one bomb.

Shirin Ebadi has met many barriers in her life, but true to the patterns of her childhood, she has unswervingly striven to surmount them even if it has meant threats and prison. She has gone forward with confidence into territories where no other woman in Iran had gone before. Although she has no wish to be a role model, we can only be grateful that such human beings are on the earth working for justice. The calling she felt as a child, the call to defend the weak, has been fulfilled a hundredfold.

5

Adolfo Pérez Esquivel
Disappeared but not Forgotten

Born in 1931 in Buenos Aires, Adolfo Pérez Esquivel was educated as an artist and city planner, becoming a professor first in La Plata and later in Buenos Aires. Inspired by Gandhi, Marin Luther King and Helder Cámara ("a mystic in love with the poor"), in the early 1970's Pérez Esquivel became active organizing nonviolent actions in support of the poor and against the arms race. After twenty-five years of dedicated university teaching, in 1976 the new military dictatorship in Argentina relieved him of his duties as a professor of sculpture at the University of Fine Arts in Buenos Aires. Between its takeover in 1976 and its downfall in 1983 the military junta practiced a "DirtyWar" against its own people, "disappearing" thousands who voiced opposition to them or their policies.

In 1977 while processing his passport, Pérez Esquivel was suddenly arrested and imprisoned without trial. They attempted to "disappear" him as well. Only after fourteen months and much local and international pressure was he released from prison. He has described his experiences while under arrest in powerful language in his book, *Christ in a Pancho*:

. . .

Certain things took on a special meaning for me. I was arrested on April 4 — the Monday of Holy Week. It was the anniversary of the death of Martin Luther King, Jr., too. So I had quite a special Holy Week that year. It started with thirty-two days in what they call "the Pipe" — a very narrow, L-shaped cell just long enough for a prisoner to lie down in, with a little space at the door to stand up in.

For the first two days in the Pipe it was completely dark. On the third day the guards opened the door and the light came in. All of a sudden I could see dozens and dozens of graffiti — names of dear ones, prayers, insults, all sorts of things. Scribbled across some of the prayers was, "In the evening of your life you'll be judged on your love," and, "Holy Virgin, we're innocent," and, "Father, forgive them for they know not what they do."

But what struck me most was a huge bloodstain, and an inscription below it scrawled by somebody's finger dipped in the blood: "God doesn't kill." Ever since, that inscription has remained engraved somewhere on my insides. It will be there all my life! These are the things that leave their mark on you — right while you're being tortured.

But to back up a bit — I was arrested at federal police head-quarters. I had gone there to have my passport renewed. I had to have it in order to visit Bishop Proaño, since I was supposed to keep track of the work up there. But when I went into the downstairs where you usually renew passports, they told me, "Go on upstairs, they'll give it to you up there."

When I got upstairs, two policemen were waiting for me. They took me into an office, and that's where I stayed. But I had a friend with me, and he saw what happened and got out fast. He went straight to tell my wife. When she appeared on the scene, the police started to tell her they hadn't arrested me. But, she said, "How can you say that? I was right here!"

If it hadn't been for my wife, I would just be one more missing person. In fact, the papers did report, for several days, "Pérez Esquivel missing." Evidently the police didn't want to admit I had been arrested. But then my wife came back with some attorneys and declared: "I was with my husband at police head-quarters when he came to renew his passport. He was arrested here." Her firmness of mind was the determining factor.

• • •

Then what is the purpose of putting you away? Simply to destroy you. Psychologically and physically. I was in Unit Nine, in maximum security quarters. We were treated severely — constant body searches, with blows and all manner of annoyances. But the worst was to hear your comrades crying out when they were being beaten or moved to another jail. We would hear them getting out of the trucks. It would be about three or four in the morning, and we could hear the blows of the guards and the cries of the prisoners. It was awful.

Then I was tortured and thrown into the punishment cell, a real dungeon, a place they called the Sty. It was a terribly difficult time. But the worst thing, the most fearsome thing, was not the beatings they gave me or what they made me do — it was always the cries of my comrades. That was horrible, inhuman.

Prison — well, I got through it different ways. As far as I'm concerned, it's important to keep enough serenity inside you by means of prayer, to hear God's silence, you might say — hear what God's trying to tell us in our personal life and in the signs of the times, and to see how we're living the signs of the times.

What hurt Adolfo Pérez Esquivel most, he tells us, was not his own torture but the cries of others. He could hear and, one senses, feel the suffering of many around him. Such is the power of compassion that the suffering of others can be felt in us as greater than our own. The solitude of prison can drive a person mad, or it can become "God's silence." In that silence we can learn to hear beyond our own desires. In the religious language of Pérez Esquivel, through silence awareness deepens and God intimates to us the good. The signs of the times in which we live can indicate to us the means we will use to bring the good about, moving from idea to action.

I can't get the picture out of my mind; in "the Pipe" Adolfo was surrounded by scripture written a few inches from his face on the stone walls in the blood of other victims. Wrapped within these inscribed walls, he cultivated in himself the serenity required to survive the brutality of his jailers as a whole human being whose heart could reach through the walls to fellow sufferers. We would all do well to remember the words of St. John of the Cross, "In the evening of your life you'll be judged on your love."

Since his release in mid-1978 Pérez Esquivel has remained an active advocate for the rights of the poor and forgotten people of South America. In addition, he demanded proper judicial prosecution of those in the government and military throughout South America who were responsible for the death and torture of so many innocents. In 1980 he was awarded the Nobel Peace Prize. Speaking about the Prize, his thoughts turned immediately to others,

> When I was awarded the Nobel Prize for Peace, it was understood very well that I was receiving it in the name of the struggling people. It is not my personal award. I received it in the name of all the peoples of Latin America, in the name of all who have no right to speak, in the name of all who are toiling in the same cause — peasants, working people, Indians, bishops, all who are together in the same task. I am but a part of the whole, and the lot fell on me. It could have been someone else.

In a 2005 interview, PeaceJam asked Adolfo Pérez Esquivel about his greatest hopes and fears for humanity. He spoke of the need for a new type of analysis of the world situation, and then genuine action. Without action everything could be lost:

> I think that in this moment, with so many problems in the world, with wars, conflicts, hunger, social exclusion, I think that it is necessary to analyze the world's situation. An imposed neo-liberal model has been exhausted. We need to provoke change in the world away from today's situation in which an unjust and asymmetric humanity lives.

And discourse is not enough, it's not enough to send letters to governments that don't listen, they don't even read the letters. Instead, we need a strong call to humanity's conscience. Also, words need to be accompanied by actions or else they are without effect. Concrete decisions need to be made. If not we will not see these changes and we will be facing enormous challenges for the survival of humanity.

My other hope is a return to thinking about humankind's relationship with Mother Nature because we are losing Her, this little planet called Earth is being destroyed. I believe the greatest challenge for social and cultural movements is creativity and thought. I think we are at a stage of disarming "armed consciousness." If we don't manage to disarm our consciousness we are divided. Therefore the future depends on the lessons and the courage we have to have in the present. There is no other way.

What would it mean "to disarm consciousness"? How would this change the way we see and act in the world? We arm ourselves for economic and political dominance; what would the world be like if instead we practiced a politics of truth and the law of love? When asked what he would write in a letter to today's youth, Pérez Esquivel responded simply: "That they never lose hope. That there always exists a possibility and a new dawn. I would share the proverb which says that the darkest hour is right before the dawn."

6

Rigoberta Menchú Tum
Healing Ravaged Communities

Rigoberta Menchú Tum's life story is one so filled with adversity and suffering that one can hardly reconcile her compact buoyant presence with the horrors of her earlier life in Guatemala. Born in 1959 into a poor Indian peasant family, she was raised in traditions of the Quiché branch of the Mayan culture. Her childhood memories are of a small homestead in the beautiful mountains of northwest Guatemala where her family lived four months of the year, and of working on the plantations of the south coast where they picked coffee, cotton, and sugar cane for the remainder of the year. When twenty-three years old, she told her story to a European journalist who published it as *I, Rigoberta Menchú*.

> Where I live is practically a paradise, the country is so beautiful. There are no big roads, and no cars. Only people can reach it. Everything is taken down the mountainside on horseback or else we carry it ourselves. So, you can see, I live right up in the mountains. My parents moved there in 1960 and began cultivating the land. No one had lived up there before because it's so

mountainous. But they settled there and were determined not to leave no matter how hard the life was.

I grew up on the *fincas* [plantations] too. Cutting cane was usually men's work, but at certain times of the year both men and women were needed to cut cane. I had five older brothers and sisters. I saw my two eldest brothers die from lack of food when we were down in the *fincas*.

Her idyllic mountain landscape was embedded in a larger violent history of oppression. Rigoberta was born into the midst of a forty-year period of violence funded and fueled by misguided U.S. fears during the Cold War. In 1954 the C.I.A. orchestrated the overthrow of a democratically elected socialist government in Guatemala, which led to over thirty years of unrest. During this period more than 200,000 Guatemalans were slain. In the 1970s and 80s the U.S.-backed right-wing military junta turned their fury on the Mayas, razing 450 Indian villages and generating one million refugees. While the mountains were beautiful, the economic and political plight of the Mayan Indians was, in these years, desperate. Ethnic cleansing was proceeding apace, which in turn led to the formation of a guerrilla resistance movement in the mountains and rural countryside.

Rigoberta's family had become prominent leaders in the rights movement and a new farmworkers' rights union called the Committee of the Peasant Union (CUC). Soon, she lost her father in a scene of great drama and tremendous violence:

> A march on the capital was organized to demand that the army leave El Quiché. They brought many orphaned children with them as proof of the repression. They took over several radio stations to tell people about our plight. At the same time, they thought they should make it known internationally by occupying an embassy where the Ambassadors would be spokesmen. So they occupied the Spanish embassy.

> But what happened afterwards was something we could never have imagined. First, because they were important people, and second because government officials were there and they died in the fire together with the peasants. Of course we knew there would be tension, but we thought that they would give all the ones who occupied the embassy permission to leave the country as political refugees, and they would be able to spread the

news of our struggle abroad. The objective was to tell the whole world what was happening in Guatemala and inform people inside the country as well.

They were all burned to death. The only thing left was their ashes. This was a tremendous blow. What hurt me very, very much was the lives of so many *compañeros*, fine *compañeros*, who weren't ambitious for power in the least. All they wanted was enough to live on, enough to meet their people's needs. This reinforced my decision to fight, but I had to face some terrible moments.

One of our *compañeros*, Gegorio Yuja Xona, was still alive among the bodies. We managed to rescue him and take him to a private hospital for medical attention. But later he was kidnapped from the hospital by armed men, men in uniform who just calmly took him away. The next day he was left in front of San Carlos University: tortured, with bullet wounds, dead.

In all Menchú Tum lost both her parents, two brothers, a sister-in-law and three nieces and nephews to the Guatemalan security forces. Again and again, Rigoberta tells us that her story is that of her people. It is not something that she and her family endured alone, but rather it was the experience of an entire community. "I'd like to stress that it's not only *my* life, it's also the testimony of my people. My story is the story of all poor Guatemalans. My personal experience is the reality of a whole people." She was witness to the basest conduct one human being can inflict on another, becoming the spokesperson for the hundreds of thousands of voiceless poor in Guatemala who suffered the same fate as her own relatives.

In the midst of such horror, how could Rigoberta Menchú Tum consistently turn away from violence and towards nonviolence? In a PeaceJam interview she explained that she had to learn to "not only think of the death, the hate, and the rancor." Instead she redoubled her efforts in the

CUC and was a prominent figure in a 1980 farmworker strike for better conditions. The military targeted her for arrest, and it was only by constantly moving, hiding, and through the protection of trusted friends that she eluded torture and death herself. It became impossible for her to remain in Guatemala. Everywhere she went she endangered those who protected her. In 1981, she fled to Mexico.

In exile she became the world spokesperson for her people, the Guatemalan poor, and a powerful voice against the terrible oppression they suffered at the hands of the right-wing military. In 1992, Menchú Tum was awarded the Nobel Peace Prize "in recognition of her work for social justice and ethno-cultural reconciliation based on respect for the rights of indigenous peoples."

As with the other Nobel Laureates, PeaceJam asked Rigoberta Menchú Tum what her greatest hopes and fears were for the future. She spoke first about her fears concerning the human and natural disasters she saw around her:

> Well, the tragedies are already occurring. We call them natural disasters, but they are not natural disasters, and there are things that happen that are not necessarily caused by people. But I believe that participation is very important. If there is a woman sitting at home lamenting what is going on out in the streets, she is surely not going to be contributing anything. But if there is a woman who gets together with others and tries to struggle alongside them, surely she can make an impact. All the same, if the democratic system is based on election, the public has to be more conscious as to who they elect because their vote is sacred. And that capacity to mobilize the population towards participation is a very broad avenue, which we have not pursued, which we have not managed to travel. Hopefully there are young people now who are going to motivate others so they might go down this road.

There are other phenomena, like in Bolivia, and even though Evo Morales's period of government has been very short, he is creating a precedent in history. It's one where the people arise and vote and elect a person who will leave a precedent in the histories of native peoples. There is a key thing we must cultivate aside from our participation, and that is to take pride in our successes. There are successes on the part of Latin Americans, on the part of young people, and by women.

Rigoberta's hope is in people. These are words spoken by one who lacked all conventional access to power and privilege. Rigoberta Menchú Tum was poor and poorly educated, a woman in a man's culture, a Maya Indian in a society ruled by the descendants of European colonists, and a pacifist in a nation in the grip of a brutal right-wing military. And still, Menchú Tum's hope lay in people, in those of moral character and profound courage regardless of wealth, power or formal education. In the face of every adversity and cruelty, a people committed to an ideal can endure decades of violent repression until peace prevails. I take this as evidence for the power of the invisible, of the moral and spiritual dimensions of life.

Menchú Tum's work in Guatemala paralleled that of Adolfo Pérez Esquivel's in Argentina and Oscar Arias' in Costa Rica. From 1970 to 1995, Central and South America was a region beset with troubles, many of which can be traced back to the Cold War fears of the U.S. that neighboring governments might become Communist. That fear armed and trained right-wing militias, which in turn led to the oppression of millions, the destruction of hundreds of villages, and the death of many thousands. The three people from the Americas featured here represent countless others who stood firmly against fear and acted with humanity in terrible times. It is on such people and actions that a true social future can be built. Fear breeds only division and destruction.

7

Oscar Arias
Beyond Violence to True Diplomacy

When Oscar Arias was elected President of Costa Rica in 1986, the U.S.-backed Contras had created bases inside of Costa Rica's northern border from which they could launch operations against the Sandinista government in turbulent Nicaragua. Costa Rica had officially declared its neutrality in 1983, but only when Arias took the reins of power did policy become reality. He worked hard to expel the Contras and enforce strict neutrality, much to the chagrin of Ronald Reagan's U.S. government. This laid the basis for Oscar Arias' energetic work to establish peace in Central America. Although critical of the political system established by the Sandinistas, which had acted in cruel ways against the native Indian peoples of Nicaragua, Arias rejected the Reagan administration's secret and illegal CIA-led policy of violence. Instead he established a peace process, meeting with the Presidents of Guatemala, El Salvador, Honduras, and Nicaragua to work out face-to-face a peace agreement all parties could adopt. Arias' peace plan was signed by all five Central American presidents in Guatemala on August 7, 1987, which led to Oscar Arias receiving the Nobel Peace Prize that year.

• • •

Oscar Arias was a student of law, economics and political science, studying at Boston University, the University of Costa Rica, the London School of Economics, finally receiving his Ph.D. from the University of Essex in 1974 in political science. When speaking to a group of university students in Minnesota as part of a Peace Prize Forum in 1991, Arias characterized himself during his university years as an idealist.

> As I look back on my college years, it is easy to view my ideas and
> convictions as mere idealism. Perhaps "idealism" is the correct
> term. But this kind of idealism, an idealism born from a pure
> belief in the purposes of justice, is a necessary idealism. It is an
> idealism that I had to turn to, again and again, when struggling

for the pacification of Central America. It is an idealism that will permit myself and others to address the new challenges being faced in my region — the consolidation of new-found peace, democracy and human development.

Like the other Nobel Laureates, Arias recognizes not only the idealism of his own youth, but he also sees this idealism as natural to the age of university students. Arias strongly urged them to hold on to their idealism, to hold out against those that would take their idealism from them:

> You are still feeling that sense of idealism — that wholehearted belief that the world can and will change. I urge you to keep that idealism, to protect it from a world that can too often be cruel and cynical. Believe in your principles, act on their behalf — retain the idealism that will allow you to make your visions and dreams a reality for yourself and others.

In other words, we should be life-long visionaries. Oscar Arias could be speaking for all the Nobels. They have all held to their dreams and ideals, rejecting the sophisticated and cynical arguments of jaded politicians, and instead sitting down with adversaries to work out a real peace. An idealist is not naïve; many are the obstacles to peace, as Oscar Arias stated eloquently in his Nobel Peace Prize acceptance speech:

> The road toward peace is long, blocked by excessive pride, intolerance and prejudice. The road to peace can only be traveled by those who have faith in the greatness of humanity and are able to be patient and tolerant. As long as leaders lack a genuine commitment to dialogue and tolerance for international differences, there will always be the danger that a careless moment will hurl humanity into the abyss of destruction.

Although these words were spoken fifteen years ago, they ring even truer today than ever before.

• • •

Prior to the Iraq war Arias wrote thoughtfully and forcefully against military intervention in Iraq. Fully recognizing the danger Saddam Hussein represented, he nonetheless rejected the use of military force. Like Reagan's ill-conceived policy for Central America, he believed a war in the Middle East would lead to nothing good. To those same Minnesota students, he gave his frank assessment of the uses of war.

> I firmly believe that war is seldom a solution. Most often, wars create problems that are more complex and difficult than those they sought to combat. In both the moral and material sense, armed conflicts do not necessarily produce triumphant peoples or nations. They generally produce other kinds of defeat.

When PeaceJam asked Arias to speak about his greatest hopes and fears for the future he, like José Ramos-Horta, turned to the issue of poverty. He argued that now, more than ever before in human history, we have the means to address this pervasive social ill:

> I think that for the first time in many years, in the history of humanity, the world has been capable of reducing poverty, partly due to the elevated economic growth in certain parts of the planet. Fundamentally, this is due to the rapid growth of China and India, but unfortunately this is not the case in sub-Saharan Africa or Latin America. Nevertheless, I think there is an encouraging voice, a flame of hope, because nations are integrating themselves more and more; and I am one of those that think that the future ought to have more globalization and not less. For the first time in history, since 1980 to today, the world has seen a significant reduction of poverty. There's still much more that we need to do, and there is much more that wealthy nations need to do in order to achieve more justice and less inequality on this planet.

• • •

Oscar Arias believes that much more needs to be done to redress the inequities in the distribution of wealth among the world's diverse nations and peoples. Our priorities in this regard are based on our values, and it is these that we must change in a way that will serve the 21st century. In Arias's words, "We begin the 21st century and continue with a value system, which I think is wrong, full of cynicism, hypocrisy, and egoism, instead of having a new ethics for the 21st century, one with more solidarity, with more compassion, with more tolerance, with more justice, and with more love." These are Oscar Arias' lofty hopes for the future. But what are his fears?

> And finally among the fears, it's going to be very difficult eradicating terrorism if we don't simultaneously eradicate so much injustice, so much economic and social disparity in our world. On the other hand, I think that at any moment we may find ourselves with countries with nuclear weapons that are not going to be as responsible as those countries which have had nuclear weapons in the past. Soon, not only may we find ourselves with governments with nuclear weapons, but also nuclear weapons in the hands of terrorists, why not? Well, this makes us think of Einstein's expression that the fourth world war will be fought with sticks and stones because a third world war is going to leave us in ruins on this planet.

From an idealistic university student of economics and political science to president and Nobel Laureate, Oscar Arias has worked to further peace in Central America, and through his foundation he has continued to labor hard for the rights of women, for demilitarization, and for the reduction of small arms trafficking. In 2006, twenty years after his first term as Costa Rica's President, Oscar Arias was elected to a second term in that same high office. We hope that his new period as President is marked by similar historic achievements for Central America and for the world.

8

Máiread Corrigan Maguire
Building a New Culture

In 1976 Belfast and much of Northern Ireland was at the height of "the Troubles" that would kill 3,400 people before subsiding with the 1998 Good Friday accord. In 1976 Máiread Corrigan Maguire would be catapulted into the leadership of the peace movement in Northern Ireland through the tragic death of her sister's three children. Born in 1944, she and her sister had grown up together in a Catholic family, Máiread the second of seven children. Already as a teenager she was active in church groups, in particular the lay Catholic organization the Legion of Mary. In her book, *The Vision of Peace*, she remembered those early years this way:

> When I was thirteen my family moved to Andersonstown, another poor section of the Catholic ghetto. Once there, I was put in charge of a group of the Legion of Mary. In the beginning only a half-dozen adolescents belonged to our group. Later, we had as many as a hundred and fifty. We did some good work in Andersonstown in 1969 and throughout the early "troubles." We arranged to get children and some young people away from

the conflict areas in order to keep them from getting involved in the disturbances. For a long time, it was a sort of national sport to throw stones at the British troops; and I'm sorry to say, many of our children were champions at that sport. Andersonstown is one of those communities built in haste by the Government in the west of Belfast. It was designed simply to house as many people as possible, with little or no social amenities. There were a few shops, no cinemas, no playgrounds, no meeting halls, etc. Once there, you're more or less stranded. We asked for funds to build a meeting hall. When the hall was built, another girl and I organized Andersonstown's first nursery school. Then we set up a center for activities and recreation for the numerous handicapped children in the area.

• • •

Máiread had to leave school at 14 to work as a secretary and help support her family, but her volunteer work within the Legion of Mary continued unabated. During these years Northern Ireland was increasingly torn by strife. When 29 years old, the sorrow of a senseless and violent death came especially close to Máiread.

> In 1973, one of my best friends, Paddy Diego, was killed. Paddy had been the president of the Legion of Mary center at Turf Lodge, one of the Catholic sectors. After his death, I took over his center as well as my own. But I was also involved in other things. Between 1972 and 1974, the Legion of Mary was the only organization for laypeople which was allowed to visit the prisoners in the Long Kesh internment camp near Belfast. For two years, two of my coworkers and I spent our Sundays there, talking to the Catholic prisoners, listening to them, trying to understand them. I also used to visit their families. It was exacting work, but extremely satisfying.

Máiread's engagement in social work was well established by 1976. She knew all sides of the conflict: the loss of beloved friends, the stories of prisoners, the plight of wives and children left behind. Yet for all her social involvement, everything changed the day that an IRA gunman, Danny Lennon, was shot by British soldiers as he sped around a Belfast street corner. Dead at the wheel, his car plowed into three children, Máiread's nephews and niece, killing them and maiming her sister. In the next months she, journalist Ciaran McKeown, and Betty Williams spoke out on television and at rallies, organizing women and others against the insane violence that raged between Catholic and Protestant factions in Northern Ireland, and between the British soldiers and the Irish paramilitary groups. They started the Peace People, a grass-roots charity that went on to organize the largest demonstrations Northern Ireland had ever seen, walking in districts and along streets where they were told they would be shot. Refusing to give way to fear, they walked anyway. Two weeks after the loss of her sister's children a huge and diverse group gathered to march through a Protestant neighborhood. Her bright blue eyes alive with the memory, Máiread recalled the event.

> I remember the sunny day, August 28, when over 25,000 of us walked along the Shankill Road, the loyalist/Protestant neighborhood. Before this march, I received a telephone call from a nun asking me if she and some of the other nuns should come to the march wearing their religious habits or in ordinary clothes. They came in their habits, and we will never forget those nuns being hugged and welcomed by the people of the Shankill. Their welcome was warmer than the sun.

For those who witnessed it, the welcome of Catholic nuns in habit by the Protestant people of Shankill warmed them like the sun. The sight of women of different faiths embracing each other is an apt image of what it means to be a human being in relation with others. We can choose to hold one another in our times of grief instead of fueling the cycle of revenge. During the first year of their actions the level of violence decreased by 70 percent. For their work Máiread Corrigan Maguire and Betty Williams shared the Nobel Peace Prize for 1976.

After the demonstrations and the Nobel award, the media's interest evaporated, but Máiread's dedication to the cause of peace never flagged. She continued to protest violence regardless of ridicule and disinterest. She had lost three young family members and later would lose her sister to suicide. It was time for Ireland to stop killing its own. Recently, as with other Nobel Laureates, we asked Máiread to look into the future and speak to us about her greatest hopes and fears for humanity. As animated as always, she replied,

> Well, my greatest hope is that we do become what Martin Luther King called a beloved community, and I think that is possible. Because essentially, people are good and they want to do what is right, and there is a great deal going on, and we need to change

what is wrong. And I think that the voice of millions of people around the world calling for peace, calling for nonviolence, calling for a new human family is tremendously important. My fears . . . well, I'm trying to learn not to be afraid, it's a bit of a waste of energy, isn't it? Our greatest enemy is indeed fear. If we give in to fear on an individual level or on a collective level, then we will enter into a negative world. I think we have to change our mindset to be positive, and to overcome our fear, to let it go . . . It is possible. And to live every moment in the moment fully alive and loving, and I think that's good. I would hope that people around the world would not become paralyzed in fear today because it looks like there's so many problems, but rather they will be hopeful for the future, hoping together to make it better.

Her message is clear. We must learn to turn firmly away from fear, which only leads to calamitous decisions and provokes regrettable reactions or paralysis. In her own life, Máiread steadfastly has rejected fear in favor of the "beloved community" of Martin Luther King. In 1957 King declared, "The aftermath of nonviolence is the creation of the beloved community, while the aftermath of violence is tragic bitterness." The aftermath of violence in Northern Ireland was altogether too familiar to Máiread Corrigan Maguire. The loss of friends and family members had thrust upon her the bitter taste of tragedy; she knew it firsthand. Since 1976 she has turned away from fear and has turned toward nonviolent action in order to help shape a new culture of peace. It is a culture that embraces difference, one in which Catholic, Protestant, Jew and Muslim are equally brothers and sisters. It is a beloved community in which black and white, Hispanic and Asian can live together and come to love one another. Is there another vision worth holding for your whole life? Here is how Máiread Corrigan Maguire described her dream to PeaceJam:

I think we have a power in our world which is more important than nuclear weapons and nuclear power, and it is the power of love. Human beings are born to love and to be loved. It's a mystery; we don't know why this is, but they are. Whenever they take that love and combine it with an activity, that will bring change. For example, if we see where there is injustice or cruelty or war, if we bring our love to that and organize our societies to solve our problems without violence, then we can save the world. I have a dream, and my dream is to build non-killing societies. It is possible. We have somehow bought into this lie in the human mind that we have a right to kill each other, so we train people to go out there (which is totally against our human nature), and we train them to kill. This is wrong. We need now to organize our societies on a new value that we can solve our problems without killing each other. The power of love organized can solve problems. I am very hopeful of starting where we live in our communities, building non-killing societies, teaching nonviolence to our little children right from their very youth, in our homes and our schools and our communities, to solve their problems in a nonviolent way. Peer mediation, conflict resolution, we'd show them the ways so that we move away from the old lie that we have, somehow in our mind, that we have a right to kill each other. We can do it a different way.

9

José Ramos-Horta
Creating Peace and Democracy

East Timor declared independence from Portugal in 1975. For the next 25 years the small island nation was the scene of shocking oppression and brutality. Shortly after its independence, it was invaded and occupied by the Indonesian army who, despite a vicious campaign, failed to quell the Timorese people's insistence on independence and self-determination. Approximately 150,000 Timorese died in the two decades of occupation that followed the Indonesian invasion. Western powers were complicit in the oppression of East Timor, supplying arms to the Indonesian army and quietly supporting their effort. Gradually, through the efforts of José Ramos-Horta and others, the plight of the East Timorese people came to the attention of the West, and international pressure led to increased action. In 1999 the U.N. supervised a popular referendum in which a vast majority of East Timorese voted for independence. Their sufferings, however, did not end with the referendum. Throughout 1999 anti-independence Timor militias — organized and supported by the Indonesian military — practiced a scorched-earth campaign of intimidation and retribution killing approximately 1,400 Timorese, displacing 300,000 people into

West Timor as refugees, and destroying the entire country's infrastructure and economy. Only when international peacekeeping forces entered East Timor was peace finally restored. Since then reconstruction has proceeded with international assistance and, remarkably, a Commission for Truth and Friendship was established in August 2005 by the presidents of East Timor and Indonesia as a means of uncovering the truth about the terrible events of 1999 and reaching closure on that tragic period.

José Ramos-Horta's life parallels the stages of East Timor's struggle for independence. Born in 1949 in East Timor's capital city of Dili, Ramos-Horta was the son of an exiled Portuguese dissident and an East Timorese mother. He was educated in a Catholic mission school in a rural village and was himself exiled for two years by the fascist Portuguese colonial authorities for subversive speech. He describes his encounter with the Portuguese Security Police (PIDE), and the circumstances of his exile in his book *Funu: The Unfinished Saga of East Timor.*

> When I was 18, in 1970, I left Dili for exile in Mozambique. I had spent an evening carousing with an American from New Jersey and a group of Australian hippies. Under the influence of alcohol I had uttered some "subversive" statements, ridiculing the Portuguese "civilizing mission." Perhaps more serious, for a fascist regime, was my suggestion that "if Portugal is too poor to develop Timor, better give it to the Americans." For this, I was called into Portuguese security police headquarters for interrogation, which lasted six full hours. That was my first encounter with the dreaded PIDE, and I was so shaken that when a detailed report of that evening's incidents was read to me, I admitted to every charge and could only say: "I'm so sorry, I didn't mean to say all these things." The senior police officer who interrogated me, *Senhor* Biscaia, a man with a bulldog face, said: "You are done. You are burnt for the rest of your life. The only thing I envy is your age."

After his return two years later, Ramos-Horta practiced journalism and became the leader of the Timorese Social-Democratic Association, which sought independence from Portugal. The pro-independence movement recruited Ramos-Horta to be their voice abroad, and in the brief period after gaining independence from Portugal and before occupation by Indonesia, he was Minister of External Relations and Information for the first provisional government of East Timor. Three days after he left East Timor the Indonesian military invaded, the borders were sealed and Ramos-Horta was forced to live in exile for many years. During that long period he tirelessly spoke out on behalf of the thousands of displaced, imprisoned, tortured, raped and slain countrymen as Permanent Representative to the United Nations for the East Timorese independence movement. Four of his brothers and sisters were killed by the Indonesian military. The vision of their suffering kept him active as the voice of East Timor, a voice heard not only at the United Nations and abroad, but also heard at home in East Timor. When asked in 2004 if he ever considered abandoning his mission Ramos-Horta responded,

> Every time I thought of that, I felt that if I did that, I would be betraying those back in East Timor, in the jungles, in prison, who were relying on me, who were trusting me and who gave me a mandate to speak for them. My conscience was telling me that I could not find a job and earn a living, have a family while people in Timor, you know. . . innocent people were being tortured, were being killed, and they still have illusions that somehow I could get the UN to help them. And I remember, when I went back, one day I went to a village in Timor — not long ago, two years ago [in 2002] — there were hundreds and hundreds of people there, welcoming me, and I felt embarrassed. And in my speech, I told them, "I'm embarrassed — you receive me as a national hero when YOU are the ones who are real heroes, because you were here. You suffered, you endured the isolation, torture. You never gave up." And one old man, maybe in his 80s, he stood up and he said, "No, you ARE our hero because when we lost hope, we heard your voice in the radio and we had hope again." I did not realize, being outside, you know, how important my work was for them.

We often do not know the full import of our words and actions. Others may well be listening, watching, and drawing inspiration from them. Maintaining our courage even without outer support or apparent success is an essential act of faith in humanity. For his efforts, José Ramos-Horta was awarded the Nobel Peace Prize in 1996.

In February 2006 PeaceJam asked Ramos-Horta to look forward to the next ten or twenty years, and to suggest worthy goals for the world:

• • •

I would prefer to set modest goals. And I know the international community — led by countries like the United States and the Europeans, but working with other countries like India, like Brazil, China, Japan — have the resources and the know-how to eliminate poverty from the face of the Earth, maybe not completely, but we can eliminate extreme poverty, bring in clean water to villages, bring in education and information. Another goal that I would set would be working with everyone concerned, with schoolteachers, with parents, with community leaders, with church spiritual leaders to eliminate prejudice and ignorance that is easily appropriated and manipulated by demagogues to spread hatred and cause phenomena like we have today with international terrorists, that make each and every one of us uncomfortable and feel insecure in our homes or when we travel. We could set these two goals, and the two are more or less related. If people are extremely poor, if they feel they have been excluded, well, they are easily manipulated. If they are uneducated — if they have no access to education, we leave the demagogues, the religious demagogues, the political demagogues to feed them with propaganda and false information about others. So the two are interlinked. I would set those two goals and I believe we **can** defeat the forces of hatred and prejudice.

The achievement of these two goals — the elimination of poverty and prejudice — depends not so much on resources (these we have) but on leadership. If we are to find the will to reduce suffering and eliminate deep poverty from the world, leaders will need to arise throughout the world who truly care about the suffering of those distant from them. The need for leadership is as great in the sphere of education as in politics. If ignorance and prejudice are to be reduced, then, as Ramos-Horta told PeaceJam, it will require "that somewhere in the Middle East, in the Muslim world, will emerge a person like Mandela, like Martin Luther King, or the great Mahatma Gandhi who will speak out against extremism, against intolerance and lead the Middle East and other countries out of oppression, out of this cycle of violence and hatred."

The presence of such leaders is not assured. When we asked Prime Minister Ramos-Horta about his greatest fears for the future he replied,

> My greatest fear is that because of lack of vision, lack of compassion . . . because of absence of leadership in the United States, in Europe and in other countries, we are moving further and further towards alienation, towards maybe a real clash of cultures, of peoples, a clash of civilization that will see rampant violence all over the world, in the streets of Europe and in the streets of the United States. That would be an enormous tragedy and unforgivable because we have it in our hands, in our reach to change things, to make the planet and the world in twenty years from now a far better one than we are living in today.

Our times desperately need figures with the stature of Gandhi around whom millions of others can rally in support of a positive vision of the future. A movement such as this would help to end the cycle of violence and hatred which continues to fuel conflicts in the Middle East, Africa and elsewhere. I imagine not one Gandhi but many, and whoever they are, we know that such leaders begin as women and men who require education and the inspiration of moral exemplars who can guide their passion for justice and generosity toward the compassionate ideal of nonviolent action. Are we surprised that so many Nobel Peace Laureates love working with young people? In working with them, the Nobels see themselves 40 years ago, and they simultaneously see the future 40 years from now. These young people want to learn about the world more than any generation before them. While appreciating the differences, they see the world as fundamentally one, as a harmony of many voices sounding together. The clash of civilizations is not an inevitability, but to avoid it will require leadership. Maybe José Ramos-Horta's two goals are already alive in the hearts of tomorrow's Gandhis. If they are, then a great work is before us.

beloved wife, because the callous junta had long denied him and their sons visas to be with her. In 1971 when Michael and Aung San Suu Kyi were engaged, Suu had a premonition that perhaps her people would need her one day, and that she would have to respond. She was the daughter of the revolutionary leader General Aung San (Burma's George Washington), who won independence from England before being assassinated by the military. In the eight months before their marriage, Suu wrote Michael 187 letters. In them she explained that she counted on his support, "not as her due, but as a favor." Suu wrote, "I ask only one thing, that should my people need me, you would help me to do my duty to them. Sometimes I am beset by fears that circumstances and national considerations might tear us apart just when we are so happy in each other that separation would be a torment. And yet such fears are so futile and inconsequential: if we love and cherish each other as much as we can while we can, I am sure love and compassion will triumph in the end."

• • •

Although she has disappeared from the world stage physically, "the Lady" as she is described in hushed whispers by the people of Burma, has been very much on the hearts and minds of her long-suffering countrymen and -women, as well as admirers around the world.

Suu Kyi met tens of thousands of supporters when she was allowed to travel the backroads of Burma during one of her releases from house arrest in 2003. On one such road, in a town called Depayin, the regime responded to the public's support of Daw Suu and expressions of support for democracy by attempting to assassinate her. This event, which she barely escaped and from which she remains under house arrest, took place on May 30, 2003. Scores of her supporters were killed or imprisoned after her convoy was attacked that day.

Others have tried to get close to her. In 1993 Adolfo Pérez Esquivel, the Dalai Lama, Máiread Corrigan Maguire, Betty Williams, Rigoberta Menchú Tum, Oscar Arias and Bishop Desmond Tutu went together to the Thai-Burma border demanding her release. Prior to that fateful day in 2003, Jody Williams was able to spend a few hours with Aung San Suu Kyi at her home. It was an incredibly powerful experience that Jody herself will never forget.

The test of a person often comes in an unexpected moment. An oft repeated story about Aung San Suu Kyi reveals something of why she carries a second nickname, "the Iron Butterfly." A beautiful and slight woman, Suu Kyi was campaigning when she and her supporters encountered a military road block. She refused to turn around. Asking her supporters to stay behind, Suu walked alone through the crowds toward the rifles that were leveled at her. At the last moment the commanding officer overruled the orders of his captain and Suu Kyi was spared.

The central place of fear in the domination of a people, whether by force or deception, erodes the core of civil society. Excerpted from her book, *Freedom From Fear*, Suu Kyi writes, "It is not power that corrupts but fear. Fear of losing power corrupts those who wield it and fear of the scourge of power corrupts those who are subject to it." Suu Kyi reminds us of the four sources of human corruption according to Buddhism: desire, ill will, ignorance and fear. Of the four, fear is the worst because it often leads to the others. "With so close a relationship between fear and corruption it is little wonder that in any society where fear is rife corruption in all forms becomes deeply entrenched."

We may think of revolution as political or economic, but if it is to endure the true revolution lies deeper within the human being and society. According to Aung San Suu Kyi,

> The quintessential revolution is that of the spirit, born of an intellectual conviction of the need for change in those mental attitudes and values which shape the course of a nation's development. A revolution which aims merely at changing official policies and institutions with a view to an improvement in material conditions has little chance of genuine success. Without a revolution of the spirit, the forces which produced the iniquities of the old order would continue to be operative, posing a constant threat to the process of reform and regeneration. It is not enough merely to call for freedom, democracy and human rights. There has to be a united determination to persevere in the struggle, to make sacrifices in the name of enduring truths, to resist the corrupting influences of desire, ill will, ignorance and fear.

> Saints, it has been said, are the sinners who go on trying. So free men are the oppressed who go on trying and who in the process make themselves fit to bear the responsibilities and to uphold the disciplines which will maintain a free society. Among the basic freedoms to which men aspire that their lives might be full and uncramped, freedom from fear stands out as both a means and an end. A people who would build a nation in which strong, democratic institutions are firmly established as a guarantee against state-induced power must first learn to liberate their own minds from apathy and fear.

• • •

Suu Kyi's attention to the spiritual as well as the political and material dimensions of revolution is entirely characteristic of her. While under house arrest her daily regime has grown to include a long session of Buddhist meditation and study every morning. Such reflection has led her to consider the long view of life, to recognize her own mortality, and to act in the light of that fundamental reality. In a 1995 interview with PeaceJam, Aung San Suu Kyi ventured an explanation of why people act so badly toward one another.

> It might be because they are not quite aware of their own mortality. There is a bit in the Mahabarata that says that the most surprising thing in the world is that although death is all around all the time, most people act as though they'd never die. They just act as though they can do what they like and get away with it and not think of the consequences. There is some truth in it because I think that the reason why people behave so badly is because they lack vision. They do not think out the full consequence. They waste time and energy by creating so much misery for others in order to make money and have power.

> Such a person would probably say what?! He wants to live comfortably, he wants to be able to have the big house and the big car and lots of money in the bank but then, does he ever stop to think that he won't live forever? He has no idea at all how long he will live and if he will ever live long enough to spend the money he has collected.

> Others will say, "Oh! We don't want the money for ourselves, we only want to provide security for our families." Do these people stop to think how much security they can give their families just by amassing a fortune? Would it not be better if they amassed good will for their families for whatever happens, so that there will be good people to look after them? With kindness or with love or with compassion?

. . .

People behave badly because they only have a very short-term vision of life. They think of it in a very narrow sense. If they had a broader and longer-term vision of life, they would probably be less inclined to go around creating as much misery as they do.

Suu Kyi's meditations have led her to value truth and love. Her politics is a politics that speaks truth to those powers that would manipulate us through fear. Hers is a politics that feels the sufferings of others; it is a politics of compassion. This has led her to labor ceaselessly for her supporters in prison, going on hunger strikes and speaking out on their behalf. The ideas of truth and love are also part of her longing for spiritual revolution, which in her view is the only proper foundation for a genuine political revolution.

Later in the 1995 PeaceJam interview we asked Suu Kyi, if you could say one thing to the young people of the world, what would it be? She replied, "Think of yourselves as old people. Think what would you be like when you are old. If you think backwards and try to live life backwards as it were, from the old peoples' point of view to your own present stage, then I think you will value your opportunities much more. You would be much more compassionate towards older people, whom you probably think are very stupid, very narrow in their views. Think backwards. Imagine yourself in the shoes of very old people and try living backwards as Merlin was supposed to have done, instead of living from childhood to old age." From the vantage point of old age the distinction between the essential and the unessential becomes much clearer. If in our youth we had the wisdom of age and the proximate sense of our own mortality, how clear and compassionate would be our actions. Live life backward; be like Merlin. Be like Aung San Suu Kyi.

11

Betty Williams
Community Solutions

Betty Williams was born in Belfast into a working-class family in 1943. The diverse community imagined by Máiread Corrigan Maguire was the reality of Betty's family life in which a Protestant man falls in love with a young Catholic woman and risks a great deal to marry her and raise a family. Life was not easy, especially when Betty was a young teen with both her younger sister and mother to care for. In her own words, she described those years this way:

> When I was thirteen, my mother became an invalid. She was paralyzed by a stroke. I was the one who raised my sister, Margaret, who is five years younger than I; and so, we are very close. My mother is a Catholic. She comes from a family of twelve children. My father is a Protestant. He works in a butcher shop. There were five children in his family. And my mother's father was Jewish!

Every day Betty saw that love, not hatred, could flourish between Catholic, Protestant and Jew. It was not an abstract ideal of religious tolerance, but

rather the lived reality of hard work, sacrifice and loving attention that keeps a family together across great differences. And like Máiread, Betty too knew the bitter taste of hatred, violence and death associated with "the Troubles." She once recounted exactly how much they touched her:

> My family has been affected by the Troubles, just as everyone else has been. Two of my cousins were killed. My Protestant grandfather, a riveter in a Belfast shipyard, was thrown down the hold of a ship under construction because his son was marrying a Catholic girl. Even afterward, they gave him a very hard time. Bigotry didn't begin yesterday. It's been around a very long time.

Soon, another tragedy struck Betty's family. In an interview with PeaceJam, Betty told the story of an incident that still brings her to tears:

> I had a situation in my life where my cousin Danny was riddled to death with bullets. He was a pre-med student at Queens University in Belfast, and he used to work weekends in a pub to bring some money in, because it was a family of eight. He was the star of the family because he was the one with the tremendous brain. And he came home one night from work, he was putting the key in the front door and they riddled him to death with the sign of the cross, simply because he was a Catholic. He fell into my aunt's arms.
>
> I was sitting in the living room after Danny's burial and the priest came . . . None of us could think straight — the anger in me was coming out sideways, because I loved our Danny — he was six-foot-four and absolutely gorgeous. A reporter asked my auntie, "How do you feel about this?" and my auntie said, "I'm so glad I'm Danny's mother and not the mother of the man who killed him." I found that so profound.

Bullet wounds in the sign of a cross: what a perverse reversal of Christian piety. Betty's other cousin chanced to pass an abandoned car loaded with IRA explosives on his way to tend cows in a farmer's field, and was killed in a huge explosion. In Betty's words, "the Protestants killed one of my cousins, the Catholics killed the other." From petty acts of bigotry to the most heinous crimes, all executed in the name of God, these formed the sad context of life during Betty Williams' youth. From such experiences she learned the heavy price of fanaticism whether religiously or nationally motivated, and she has spoken out against these caricatures of piety ever since.

After graduating from Catholic school in Belfast, Betty took a commercial course for secretaries and went on to office work by day and waitressed by night. Betty's spunky nature was in evidence from early on, getting her into regular conflict with her boss at the restaurant.

> So far as jobs were concerned, I was never one to stay in one place forever. I liked to change, to do different things. The last job I had was as a night waitress at an inn. I was fired fourteen times — for disobedience, for being insolent to the maitre d', and so forth. It was the maitre d' who had fired me all fourteen times. I was fired practically every Saturday night, after the rush hour. During the day, I worked as a "Girl Friday" in an office of technical consultants. I had both those jobs when the peace movement began.

The peace movement began for Betty when Danny Lennon's car careened into three children. She was nearby and felt called to act, to cry out, to say "enough" of the senseless bloodshed and acts of violence enacted by all parties.

Until that moment Betty Williams had been "everywoman." That is to say, her life was like that of countless other women in Northern Ireland and the rest of the Western world. She had a basic education, was holding down two jobs — secretary and waitress — trying to make ends meet. Like everyone in Northern Ireland during the Troubles, she had come to know the pain of loss and she privately mourned the dead. Yet what distinguished her, Máiread and all the people featured in this book is that they moved from private concern to sustained public action. Betty became exceptional when she responded openly and visibly to the loss of life near her. She had been a secretary; now she was an unrelenting and vocal advocate for peace in Northern Ireland. When Máiread and Betty joined forces with journalist Ciaran McKeown and cried out their message rejecting the long history of violence, tens of thousands of other women who had suffered comparable loss and who also mourned their dead joined them. What began as three became many.

· · ·

Thirty years have passed since she began her efforts to resolve the conflict in Northern Ireland. While much progress has been made in her homeland, conflict continues unabated in many other places around the world. Given the present situation, PeaceJam asked her what her hope and fears were for humanity in the coming years. She replied,

> Well, my greatest fear at the moment is that the future looks like it's going to be pretty violent, and we have countries that are surpassing themselves in terms of terrorism and acts of terrorism camouflaged under the name of governments. They only talk about one kind of terrorism, and we should be talking about the terrorism of governments, and that's got to be stopped. That's my greatest fear.

Betty is concerned not only about isolated acts of terrorism perpetrated by radical fundamentalists. On many occasions she has spoken frankly about the special responsibility of governments and indeed all civilized countries to act according to the very highest standards of ethics on the international stage.

Concerning her greatest hopes, Betty answered quickly. "Well, the hope for me? That's an easy one. Because I see the hope as being with the young people, and I know, because I'm with young people on very regular occasions, that they're very displeased with the way their world is going at the moment. They desperately want to change that. So, if there's hope to be had, it'll come through the youth." One of the first hopeful indications is an awakening to the real situation of our time, and Betty sees young people around the world dissatisfied with what they see and working to make it better. Foremost in Betty Williams' mind is the Iraq War and a way to reach an end to the violence there:

> I see people now in the United States, I think they're finally waking up to the effect of the Iraqi War. I know they're certainly waking up in Britain to what this war has done. Once we get

that floodgate closed and the insanity of what's happening in the Middle East solved, then what's happening now could very well be a cleansing. Unfortunately, hundreds of thousands of people are dying while this cleansing's going on. We have to learn to live together and stop destroying each other.

The guns, missiles and bombs are all instruments of terrible destruction aimed at human beings like us. What is the force that can neutralize these forces of death? According to Betty Williams, "The only force which can break down those barriers is the force of love, the force of truth, soul-force..." Confronted with violence, she would have us meet it with the inner soul-force of truth and love. Her words could be those of Aung San Suu Kyi.

12

Wangari Maathai
Greening Africa

When asked how her interest in the environment began, Wangari Maathai often recounts a story from her childhood in Kenya, where she and her family lived near a life-giving stream of water. In her acceptance speech for the 2004 Nobel Peace Prize, she told that story but also linked it to a crucial task before which we stand as stewards of the Earth:

> As I conclude, I reflect on my childhood experience when I would visit a stream next to our home to fetch water for my mother. I would drink water straight from the stream. Playing among the arrowroot leaves I tried in vain to pick up the strands of frogs' eggs, believing they were beads. But every time I put my little fingers under them they would break. Later, I saw thousands of tadpoles: black, energetic and wriggling through the clear water against the background of the brown earth. This is the world I inherited from my parents. Today, over 50 years later, the stream has dried up, women walk long distances for water, which is not always clean, and children will

never know what they have lost. The challenge is to restore the home of the tadpoles and give back to our children a world of beauty and wonder.

Born in 1940 in Nyeri, Kenya, Wangari Maathai came to the United States for her college education as part of a Kennedy administration program to help the then new post-colonial nations of Africa educate their young adults. This experience proved decisive for Wangari Maathai. She graduated in 1964 from Mount St. Scholastica College in Atchison, Kansas, and then went on to complete a Master of Science in biological sciences at the University of Pittsburgh, USA, and her doctoral studies in Germany and Kenya, obtaining her Ph.D. in Anatomy in 1971 from the University of Nairobi. Whereas Shirin Ebadi was the first woman to become a judge in Iran, Wangari Maathai was the first woman in eastern and central Africa to earn a Ph.D. By 1976, she was Chair of the Department of Veterinary Anatomy at the University of Nairobi, the first woman in the region to attain this and other positions. During the late 1970's while active in the National Council of Women in Kenya, Maathai developed the initiative for a broad-based women's environmental movement which focused on the planting of trees. This effort became the Green Belt Movement in 1977. Since then the Green Belt Movement has helped women's groups to plant over 30 million trees on farms, around schools and in family compounds, thereby improving the environment throughout Kenya. In the late 1980's the Green Belt Movement broadened its reach to become pan-African with grass-roots environmental initiatives in over 30 African countries and beyond.

In over 20 countries the Green Belt Movement uses tree planting as part of a civic education that empowers people, "to give them a sense of taking their destiny into their own hands, removing their fear, so that they can stand up for themselves and for their environmental rights." The problems of a village or group are listed, and instead of lamenting the lack of government assistance, Maathai suggests taking direct action.

• • •

Protecting the environment is vital, and you cannot protect the environment without dirtying your hands, without getting involved. You cannot just talk about it. In the final analysis, wherever we are, whether we are in developed countries or developing countries, we really have to get involved in action. We can talk all day, but I tell people, until you have taken an action that could make a difference, even if it is to stop water running — that's an action; planting a tree — that's an action; reusing a bag instead of throwing it; these are actions that all of us can practice, and it has to become a way of life.

Wangari Maathai's activism has not been limited to planting trees. For example, she and others protested energetically when the Kenyan President proposed to build a 62-story skyscraper in the middle of Nairobi's last undeveloped park complete with a four-story statue of himself, a monument to his vanity. On this and subsequent occasions Wangari Maathai and her compatriots in civic protest have been exposed to danger, have been arrested and even beaten. Such actions call for overcoming the fear that can so easily paralyze us.

If you don't have good governance, it is easier to exclude others, it is easier to dominate, it is easier to exploit your own and other people's resources. And so if you look, you always see that below the politics and even below the religious undertones, the real issue is who is in charge of the resources and who is being excluded. How are they reacting, for it is in that reaction that we see conflict. This happens whether it is within small nations or big nations, and so this is something we need to understand as citizens, and we need to force our politicians and our leaders to understand because they're the ones at the end of the day that make the decisions that could make a difference.

When something is not right in life, it is crucial to recognize it and to take control of the direction one is heading. One can begin locally with the simple act of planting a seedling in a barren landscape, or a group may challenge powerful forces that are tyrannizing a country. In both cases the emphasis is on reclaiming control of your own actions and thus of your own life. Complaining is not sufficient. A focused mind, a compassionate heart, and the will to act in alignment with what one knows is right, these can work miracles. They have in Kenya through the example and leadership of Wangari Maathai.

PeaceJam recently asked Wangari Maathai what her greatest hopes were for the future. She replied,

> Well, my greatest hope is that more and more people, and especially more and more young people and people in leadership — people who are making decisions — will become aware of how indeed we are dependent on the resources of this planet. And if we don't manage these resources responsibly and accountably, and if we don't prevent conflict by sharing them more equitably, our future generations will be threatened. So my hope is that these groups of people, more and more of us, therefore, will become aware of the need for us to protect the environment in every way possible, whatever we can do within the position that we occupy in our lives. They need for us to have a holistic approach, and it is mainly the leaders who can make the difference because they can introduce policies that will ensure that all of us are given the ability to protect the environment.

And when you look into the future, what is your greatest fear?

> Well, I guess my greatest fear is that we may not wake up in time, that we may not do this in time. Because unfortunately, scientists can only tell us what they are observing, and sometimes it takes a long time for decision makers to actually appreciate what scientists are telling us. For example, with respect to climate change, politicians who are in charge of countries are

sometimes too slow to appreciate that they may have to make very painful decisions so as to protect our long-term interests rather than be preoccupied with our short-term interests. So, for me, the fear is that it takes so long. Environmental degradation is a very slow process for the eyes of a human being, for the short life span we occupy. So quite often, we do a lot of damage within our own lifetime and it is only the future generation that will suffer or will pay the price for the mistakes we make within our own lifetime. That's my fear.

Wangari Maathai has recognized that to truly change environmental policy, consciousness of people must be raised to a higher level, one that "moves them to do the right things for the environment because their hearts have been touched and their minds convinced." Outer policy reflects interior values. Viewed from the outside, her life has been spent planting trees and helping many thousands of women and men to do the same. But when viewed from the inside she has been reshaping the hearts and minds of millions who now see the nakedness of a barren landscape as if for the first time, and who then find in themselves the place of action to do something about it. An interviewer once asked Maathai if she ever visited the first tree she planted. "Yes," she said laughing, "yes, the very first tree is still there. It is a big tree now, in the middle of a market. Occasionally I go and look at it, and it's doing fine." Small acts can carry great consequences.

In Memoriam

Sir Joseph Rotblat
(1908–2005)

In 2003 when Sir Joseph Rotblat was working with the young people of PeaceJam, they asked him to tell them about his life. The story he told in response spanned over ninety years from the time of his childhood in Poland before and during the First World War, to his work as a nuclear physicist on the first atom bomb in Britain and later Los Alamos, New Mexico. The story concluded with a description of his decades of work to end war and especially to eliminate nuclear weapons. He declared to the PeaceJam youth, "At the present time, the main danger is the existence of nuclear weapons." For the leadership he provided in reducing the risk of nuclear holocaust, he and the organization he helped to found — the Pugwash Conferences on Science and World Affairs — received the Nobel Peace Prize in 1995. With his death in 2005, the world, and the young people who took to him so immediately, lost a human being who combined brilliance in science with humane values of the highest order. Before turning to the conversation among twelve of the PeaceJam Laureates, it is fitting to pause to remember one of those who contributed so much to peace over a period of three generations. How fitting that in his last years he worked

with the youth of PeaceJam. We trust that his infectious enthusiasm and vision will inspire a younger generation to carry his work forward.

Serving through a Humane Science

Joseph Rotblat was a child of five when the First World War broke out in Poland. It was not long before the collapse of Poland plunged most of the population into illness and hardships. In his words, "Everything was lost, and we found ourselves in real privation, and I mean it literally, literally hunger, not enough to eat, freezing cold conditions, diseases — I was exposed to all types of diseases imaginable, squalor; it's difficult to imagine how bad it was, and these were my formative years as a child." The effect on Rotblat was profound; "it completely changed the rest of my life." From the squalor, poverty, and human suffering that he and millions of others endured, came his commitment to help change the world. In his case, he longed to help as a scientist.

Because his parents could not maintain him at school, Rotblat went to a vocational school to learn to become an electrician. After completing his vocational studies, he worked all day as an electrician and made time in the evenings for his private study of physics at home. In 1928, Rotblat successfully passed the entrance examinations for the Free University of Poland in Warsaw, where he attended lectures in the evening, graduating in 1932. In the same year, he began working for the Polish director of the Radiological Laboratory of the Warsaw Scientific Society, Professor Ludwick Wertenstein, who was previously an assistant of Maria Sklodowska-Curie. In 1939 he took a fellowship to work in England with the Nobel laureate James Chadwick. As Rotblat was about to leave Poland, he read Lise Meitner's research concerning the fission of uranium and quickly realized its significance. As he explained in a PeaceJam interview, he realized that "if this worked and if a very large amount of energy came out in a short time, then this would be a mighty explosion, an explosion of a very large amount of energy released in a very short time. In other words, one of my ideas was the atom bomb."

Working on weapons would normally have been against his moral principles, which held that science should be used for the good. "I always considered myself to be a humanitarian scientist, and by this I mean that while the main purpose of science is to pursue knowledge, to find out new things in the universe, I felt that science would also have a practical application — it should serve to remove the misery in which so many people in the world live, to provide a better world for all of us." But World War II was about to break out and Hitler was in power in Germany. Rotblat told the story himself to PeaceJam youth.

To Work on the Bomb, or Not?

If the bomb can be made and should Hitler acquire the bomb, then this would be the end of democracy as I understood it to be. So during the next few months in the summer of 1939, I lived in agony with the quandary before me — what should I do? On one hand, working on a weapon of mass destruction goes against all of my ideals about science. On the other hand, if the bomb could be made, then all of these ideas would go overboard if Hitler actually should master the world. So I found myself stuck between the devil and the deep blue sea.

As it often happens the decision was made for me by other external events — in this particular case, the external event was the outbreak of the Second World War on the first of September, 1939. It started with the invasion of Poland (my home country) by Germany; within a few weeks, Poland was defeated. The whole view of the might of Germany stood revealed, and I thought that if in addition Hitler was to have the bomb, then we could say goodbye to democracy and this was not acceptable to me. This is the reason I went to Chadwick who was the head of the department, and I suggested to him that we should begin to start work on the atom bomb.

In reaching this decision, I thought that I had not abandoned my humanitarian principles. On the contrary, I used this rationale for preventing such a catastrophe. I thought, if the bomb can be made, and if Hitler should acquire it, then the only way in which we could stop Hitler from using it against us or against the rest of the world would be if we also had the bomb and threatened him with retaliation. In other words, I conceived of the concept of nuclear deterrence, which is now still being used as an excuse for keeping nuclear arsenals. This concept I developed in the summer of 1939, and this is why I went to Chadwick suggesting to him that we should start work. Because if this view was correct, then we should have the bomb as soon as possible.

The main purpose for those people who started to work on the atom bomb was to prevent its use. Now I want you to remember the only reason that I felt the bomb needed to be made was as a deterrent so that it should not be used. However, this was not the case. The bomb was used as soon as it was made, and it was used against civilian populations.

Leaving the Manhattan Project

Rotblat worked first in England and then in the USA on the Manhattan Project to develop the atomic bomb. He described the circumstances which made him change his mind about the work.

> Chadwick told me in November 1944, that the Germans were no longer working on creating an atom bomb, so I said, "Fine, well, in this case, there's no need for me to be here." The only reason I was there was because I was afraid the Germans may have it. This turned out not to be true, and I told Chadwick, I wanted to resign. I wanted to leave and go back to England. He was not very happy about it, but he had to accept my decision. And then it turned out it was not as easy as I thought to leave the project. In order to keep me there, the American Intelligence developed a fantastic story for the reason why I wanted to leave — namely that I wanted to give away the secrets of the bomb to the Russians, that I was a Soviet spy. And the story was a fiction, a fantasy. I managed to show to them that the story was completely false, so they let me go. But, I had to agree to a condition — namely that I would not tell people the real reason — I would not tell my colleagues on the project the real reason I wanted to leave. They didn't want it to demoralize them. I should have no further contact with anybody working on the project. Only under those conditions was I allowed to leave.

> So I went back to England in December 1944. I learned about the progress that had been made on the project in August —

August 6, 1945, when I heard on the BBC Radio the announcement about the destruction of Hiroshima. This was the first time that I learned that the project I had initiated had been successful. It came as a terrible shock to me, because I still hoped that first of all maybe it wouldn't work at all, and secondly if it did work, that it would not be used against civilian populations (rather, not to be used at all, as I mentioned before), and here I find it had. This had a rather big effect on my own life.

I decided that day to change my whole line of research, and I went into medical research, which gave me much more satisfaction, but my leaving had no effect of course on the work on the Manhattan Project. Many scientists who stayed on the project were very unhappy about the way things were going, and they decided to try to use their influence to prevent the use of the bomb. The Danish scientist Niels Bohr, one of the great scientists of the century, foresaw the dire consequences of Americans using the bomb against civilian populations. He foresaw that if the Americans could make the bomb, then the Russians too could make it, and then there would be an arms race starting between the two. He predicted, in an uncanny prophecy, the nuclear arms race. In fact, what happened a few years later was that both sides, both superpowers, the United States and the Soviet Union, built huge nuclear arsenals.

So what came out from this is a stupid arms race that may lead to the destruction of the human race. This is the conclusion we've come to in the nuclear age: the human species is an endangered species. Having come to this conclusion, therefore, we have to do something about it.

Reducing the Nuclear Threat

Immediately Rotblat became active in efforts to reduce or eliminate nuclear weapons. He was the youngest of the eleven signatories of the

Einstein-Russell Manifesto issued in 1955 at the height of the Cold War. Within days the philanthropist Cyrus Eaton offered the eleven support for their initiative. From this arose the important Pugwash Conferences in which Rotblat was central. As Rotblat explained:

> The Pugwash movement was an expression of the awareness of the social and moral duty of scientists to help prevent and over-come the actual and potential harmful effects of scientific and technological innovations. At this point, many people believe that Pugwash can be described as the social conscience of scientists. We met in small groups, expert people who knew how to deal with the problems very well. In those days of the Cold War, there was a real danger that the Cold War would turn into a "hot war" in which nuclear weapons would be used. And we found that the way to prevent it from happening was by having a number of very short-term measures that would act as a brake in this race, to slow it down, and eventually bring it to a halt. This is what we invoked, a number of such short-term meas-ures. One of those measures was, for example, the Partial Test Ban Treaty in early 1963, which stopped atmospheric testing — tests just went underground, but it stopped radioactivity from coming out and harming many people in the world. The Treaty of Tlatelolco specified that Latin America should not have nuclear weapons. Then, there was the Non-Proliferation Treaty in 1968. In all of this, Pugwash played a very important role.

> Pugwash is strongly committed to the goal of abolishing all nuclear weapons. It is imperative that Pugwash constantly remind the international community of the immorality, illegal-ity, and peril inherent in nuclear weapons, and to propose con-crete steps towards their elimination.

> Now, as a result of this, our efforts were partially successful. The nuclear arms race came to a halt — it was stopped by the decision

of a new Russian leader, Mikhail Gorbachev, who told us that he listened to our advice.

Unfortunately, over the past few years and to Sir Joseph Rotblat's great dismay, weapons began to be developed in countries around the world. In his final days, Sir Joseph Rotblat led the international outcry against this change in direction and he continued to hold scientists up to a brave new standard.

> The Pugwash Conferences on Science and World Affairs are first and foremost an organization of scientists. This makes them one of the clearest manifestations of the independent social and moral responsibility of scientists for what they, and they alone, are capable of developing. Even today, recognition of that responsibility is not a matter of course. The message from Pugwash to science is a double one: it must engage actively in the struggle against the harmful consequences of earlier scientific discoveries, and it must assess in advance the consequences of new ones. Modern science is taking enormous strides. The idea of moral responsibility may be more relevant today than ever before.

In his 1995 Nobel Peace Prize address, Joseph Rotblat concluded with words that are also a fitting close to our remembrance of him.

> The quest for a war-free world has a basic purpose: survival. But if in the process we learn how to achieve it by love rather than by fear, by kindness rather than by compulsion; if in the process we learn to combine the essential with the enjoyable, the expedient with the benevolent, the practical with the beautiful, this will be an extra incentive to embark on this great task. Above all, remember your humanity.

Part Two

A Gathering of Peacemakers

Having introduced each of the PeaceJam Nobel Laureates, we are now ready to bring them together for an imaginary living room conversation. In it each will speak to the themes they care about most deeply and for which they have worked so consistently. Yet the questions I will pose to them are intended to move them beyond the particular causes to which each has given a lifetime — I will attempt to engage them in a collective search for the deeper causes of conflict and suffering as well as the wellsprings of social healing and renewal. By coming together in this way, we are hoping to discover the common chord or single voice that finds such diverse expression in the unique work of these individuals.

The words the Nobel Laureates are speaking in this conversation are largely drawn from a series of PeaceJam One Voice interviews in which exactly such probing questions were put to them. This "global conversation" was conducted over the course of twelve months, beginning in August of 2005. In other instances I have drawn from their published writings and speeches, but in all cases the words are their own, only the arrangement is mine. It is now time for our imagined conversation. I think that I hear them coming into the room...

13

Seeking the Root Causes of Conflict and Suffering

The preparations for this imagined conversation had been extensive, but finally everything was set for the gathering. It was the first time all twelve Nobel Laureates from PeaceJam were joined together. As they came into the lovely but simply appointed room, many of them embraced each other warmly, giving greetings and expressing joy at the prospect of spending the next three days together. The Dalai Lama and Desmond Tutu were smiling broadly and laughing; they were old friends who were glad to see each other. Rigoberta Menchú Tum was present in a beautiful Mayan-weave dress and was speaking with Shirin Ebadi and Jody Williams about their work together in the newly launched Nobel Women's Initiative. The founders of PeaceJam, Dawn Gifford Engle and Ivan Suvanjieff, mingled with everyone, making sure they were well cared for, as well as reminiscing together about many of the PeaceJam events they had held with the Nobels around the world.

When Aung San Suu Kyi finally entered the room, all conversation stopped and a warm sustained applause greeted her. She, who has suffered for so long under house arrest, was a special guest at the gathering, at least in all of our minds. As we all clapped, the small, slender Lady of Burma paused to serenely survey the gathering, real joy in her eyes. When she bowed to us, everyone in the room became silent; some bowed in return, some simply stood, but all of us ached from the joy in our hearts. After this exchange of respect and appreciation, everyone circled her, and one by one Aung San Suu Kyi greeted us all like true friends.

For those whose lives had, for decades, been dedicated to reducing global conflict and suffering through the widest range of actions imaginable, this was a rare occasion, one to be relished. Even though all those present had been working for peace, they had never met together in this way before. I had been asked to facilitate the gathering, so I gradually urged them to be seated in the chairs provided around a large round low coffee table. I began with the following words,

"Dear friends, if I may call you all that, we are here because we care deeply about the future, and also because we recognize the importance of youth in carrying the responsibilities for that future. Each of you has been an active part of PeaceJam, and in that role you have worked with young people all over the globe concerning the great issues and trials the Earth and humanity currently confront. Over the coming days we will engage these issues, but even more we will seek behind them. We will look beyond the individual crises to their root causes, and we will seek as well for sources of social healing and renewal. We will attempt to come to a collective insight into the needs of our time, and express that insight in ways that young people may be able to hear and act upon.

"Before starting our first session, I would like to open the gathering by asking that we enter together into the spacious sanctuary of silence, and that each of you in your own way, pray or meditate, that wisdom will enter our words and goodwill come from our work. Also, it seems appropriate to remember our departed and beloved PeaceJam colleague, Sir Joseph Rotblat, whose death in truth has not taken him from us. We know that his spirit is here with us today."

· · ·

From my earlier meetings with some of the Nobels, and from my reading of their work, I knew that they all possessed a reflective nature and spiritual depth. During the silence, that depth became palpable. I broke the silence with a quiet "Thank you." As I looked about the circle I could see that Archishop Desmond Tutu had something to say, so I invited him to speak.

"First of all," said Tutu, "I want to commend Dawn and Ivan for the incredible initiative they showed in helping to found PeaceJam. It seemed a crazy idea at the time when they started, but it has gained an incredible kind of momentum and has made a huge, huge difference in the lives of many young people in giving them hope and direction. I, myself, have very great hope for the world. We face enormous problems — there is hunger, there's conflict, there is poverty; we particularly in Southern Africa are being devastated by the HIV/AIDS pandemic, and in a way, you almost want to say there is no hope, the world is going down the tubes. But I think, 'No!' There are these fantastic people, the young people, especially, who dream dreams, and I think that is one of our greatest hopes — young people who are idealistic, who really do believe that the world can become a better place. So it is young people — not exclusively — but it is largely young people who have usually demonstrated against war, who have demonstrated against international institutions that seem to favor the affluent, and they are saying, 'This world can become a better place. This world can become a place that is hospitable to peace, to justice, to compassion.' And so, I dream that one day we will help to actualize, to bring to reality, the dream that young people have, which is God's dream, that we will come to realize that we are family, we belong together." Betty Williams leaned forward and followed on immediately, recalling the very first PeaceJam event in Denver ten years earlier.

"I say this with great pride, and maybe pride shouldn't be in it at all," started Betty, "but I was the first Laureate to do a PeaceJam and I will never forget that experience until the day that God calls me home. Because there I had a room full of young people that I could talk to at a level that they understood.

I was a ghetto child in Northern Ireland, from a Catholic ghetto, so I know what the ghetto life is all about. I will never forget that first PeaceJam in Denver, Colorado, at Regis University, where at the end of it there were several children that came over to me and said, 'You have changed the way I think — you have changed the way I look at things.' Maybe that is a God-given gift, and I know it is, because if I wasn't talking about a cause, I'd never get up in public to talk at all. Before I go up to do a PeaceJam, I go away and I pray for a little, sometimes not as long as I need to, but to say 'Thy will be done' not 'My will be done' and I get up and do it. I always ask God for one child in the room, just one — just give me one today. And PeaceJam's now worldwide.

"I remember Dawn and Ivan ten years ago coming to my house in Huntsville and I remember saying to Ivan, 'You don't know what you've gotten yourself in for. This is going to spread like wildfire.' And yet, we have the opportunity, if we're honest with the children, to turn their lives completely around. I did a PeaceJam Slam a couple of weeks ago in Minnesota with children in jail. I was so moved by the event that I had to keep going out of the room just to cry. Every child, I hugged every one, and there were 400 of them. If you're lucky enough for God to allow you to do that, you do feel that you're accomplishing something. I think that PeaceJam is the greatest gift to young people of any organization that I work for — even my own organization. With PeaceJam, it reaches hundreds of thousands of youths and it changes them profoundly. I was with a young man, Rudy Balles, who was in a gang — he's tough as nails, tattoos all over, but he's one of the most loving human beings you could ever care to meet. PeaceJam did that. Rigoberta Menchú Tum did that."

I too could recall that first PeaceJam, and Betty's remarkable way of working with every kind of young person, whether from a street gang or a suburb. They eventually all fell under her spell. Others round the circle added their thanks to Dawn and Ivan for the steadfast and dedicated work they had done during the last decade. PeaceJam had, indeed, made a difference in the lives of many young people, and all those in the room looked forward to continuing the work in the years ahead. After this warm affirmation, I turned us to the task at hand, and put to them directly the question concerning the root causes of conflict and suffering.

"There are so many problems facing the world right now, and several of you have talked about how we're always dealing with the symptoms and treating things at a surface level. You have expressed the need to seek the root causes of these problems. In your opinion, considering everything that's happening on the planet, what is the root cause of the problems we're facing?" Jody Williams responded without a moment's hesitation, "Greed." I asked her to expand.

"Well, I think it's greed. I think it's lust for power. You combine those . . ." Jody wagged her head as if to say, "you have disaster on your hands". "And when I say greed, I mean not just personal greed — political greed, governmental greed for control of the resources of the world in order to have the most power." Jody paused for a moment and shifted to the proper role of government.

"If we don't change what government really should be, I think that we won't be able to address the root causes of the problems. I think government is supposed to be an expression of the needs of the people. The government is supposed to respond to the needs of the people in the sense of the common good, not one little bunch of people from a country, but for the common good. But I don't think government does that, I really don't think too many do — there might be one or two. But as long as countries are fighting with each other for control of resources, for power, how will we ever address the root causes?"

What Role for Ignorance?

Shirin Ebadi inserted her views succinctly. "I see the root cause of these problems in basically two things: first, ignorance, and second, prejudice. We're not conscious of different religions and civilizations, and as a result we think that we are the only ones who are right. If we would do away with ignorance and prejudice, I believe we can solve many of our problems. We must start from the elementary school; we must teach our youth; we must teach them during their formative years to become lovers of peace; otherwise when they become 40 years old it may be too late to preach to them and hope to change their ideas."

"Thank you, Shirin," I responded. "I would like to hold the issue of education for a moment and ask others about your emphasis on ignorance and prejudice." Jody Williams nodded her head and responded with considerable passion:

"Ignorance. Willful ignorance, I think, is one of the biggest threats to our future. You know the ridiculous statement, 'Ignorance is bliss'? Sometimes, ignorance is bliss. It's not always fun to think about the problems of the world. But most often, ignorance is only ignorance. And if you keep yourself ignorant, then you cannot be an agent of positive change. And if you hide in your ignorance, you abdicate your own possibilities of being a productive agent of change. I think we really need to deal with the basic ignorance of humanity, and I don't mean their education. I mean, the ignorance about, what is humanness? We have to deal with that ignorance. We have to deal with the ignorance of the distortion of religion such that, it really becomes a political tool. That kind of ignorance I find probably the most oppressive of all. I think religion can be a very powerful positive agent, but throughout history it has been twisted and used so many times for oppression and more. It's a huge ignorance that we have to battle, especially in today's world."

I interjected briefly, "Some have suggested that we are in a period of world history in which we are called to battle evil. Is that true?"

At this point Aung San Suu Kyi added her thoughtful reflections to the conversation. "I once listened to a radio program about Karl Popper and he was asked the question, 'Do you believe in evil?' and he said, 'No, but I believe in stupidity.'" At this point there were smiles all around the room.

"And I agree very much with him there. I don't think that there is such a thing as evil, but I think there is such a thing as ignorance and the root of all evil is ignorance. The more you understand, the broader your vision, the broader your understanding is of the world around you, the less room there is for evil. So I do not believe in evil. I think there are such things as stupidity, as Karl Popper put it, or ignorance, as the Buddhists would put it; ignorance of what is right and what is wrong, and also, the ignorance of other people's feelings. I suppose you could call it a lack of empathy. If you could feel for others as you would feel for yourself, then there's very little room for evil, because mostly, evil is what you do to others."

Aung San Suu Kyi's articulation of the Buddhist understanding of suffering and empathetic understanding prompted the Dalai Lama to say, "I also believe that suffering is caused by ignorance, and that people inflict pain on others in pursuit of their own happiness or satisfaction. Yet true happiness comes from a sense of inner peace and contentment, which in turn must be achieved through cultivation of altruism, of love, of compassion, and through the elimination of anger, selfishness and greed."

To which Aung San Suu Kyi added, "I think that those who abhor each other are basically those who feel insecure. They feel threatened by what is different, whether it's a different color, or a different religion, or a different belief. So one would say that they have no inner confidence, no inner serenity. It's a lack of spiritual development. People who are spiritually developed do not think of others in terms of their differences, but in terms of what they have in common.

"It is not power that corrupts but fear. Fear of losing power corrupts those who wield it and fear of the scourge of power corrupts those who are subject to it. Most Burmese are familiar with the four a-gati, the four kinds of corruption. Chanda-gati, corruption induced by desire, is deviation from the right path in pursuit of bribes or for the sake of those one loves. Dosa-gati is taking the wrong path to spite those against whom one bears ill will, and moha-gati is aberration due to ignorance. But perhaps the worst of the four is *bhaya-gati*, for not only does *bhaya*, fear, stifle and slowly destroy all sense of right and wrong, it so often lies at the root of the other three kinds of corruption.

"Just as *chanda-gati*, when not the result of sheer avarice, can be caused by fear for want or fear of losing the goodwill of those one loves, so fear of being surpassed, humiliated or injured in some way can provide the impetus for ill will. And it would be difficult to dispel ignorance unless there is freedom to pursue the truth unfettered by fear. With so close a relationship between fear and corruption it is little wonder that in any society where fear is rife, corruption in all forms becomes deeply entrenched."

From Fear to Freedom

Ignorance was understood by these Nobels as the root of evil and the source of suffering. Certainly they are not speaking merely about illiteracy or the lack of relevant information. Rather it seemed to me that they were pointing to a profound structural misperception of reality that many people have. You have certainly had the experience of mistaking one thing for another, or completely misjudging a person's character. With the appearance of some new information, suddenly the entire scene changes; an enemy becomes a friend, an inscrutable problem abruptly is solved. I wanted to return to this topic later, but the theme of fear was definitely in the room and I needed to continue that discussion. Each of the Nobel Laureates had confronted fear; each had experienced death threats, the torture of loved ones or themselves. From the joy and verve they bring to life, one might never guess the force of oppression that weighed heavily on the lives of these men and women, or on their families and friends. Each one had learned to deal with fear, so I asked them to speak about it.

Shirin Ebadi started off the discussion by saying, "Any person who pursues human rights in Iran must live with fear from birth to death, but I have learned to overcome my fear."

• • •

Máiread continued reflectively, "Well, I think that each one of us, inside ourselves, we have a lot of conflicting emotions. We have fear and anger, and if we feed those negative emotions within ourselves, the fear and anger and revenge, then they can go on to become hate and that can turn into violence. Essentially from when children are very young, we need to help them learn to cope with these inner emotions, this war that is going on within themselves, so that they grow up with the attitude that their problems can be solved in a different way. Fear is very, very important, because we are all afraid. We are afraid of different things. Some people are afraid to get out of bed, because life is very hard for them. Some people are afraid to speak to someone who is a different race, a different color. Some people are afraid that their home is going to be attacked. What we have got to learn first in our own selves is how to overcome our fear, and then we can reach out to each other. A lot of conflict, war and violence starts through people being afraid. They demonize another country, and then once you have demonized them, it is easy to attack them and go to war. So we have to learn to cope with this inner fear, and I think that is very important on an individual level, on a community level, and on a world level — to deal with the fear in a positive way."

Adolfo Pérez Esquivel picked up her strain of thinking, immediately saying, "Mahatma Gandhi said that fear paralyzes, and to go from fear to safety there is only one path. The important thing is to overcome your fears, to not lose the condition of being human. And if one loses the condition of being human, then one loses their very own freedom. I think that youth should never lose the feeling of freedom, because without freedom, you don't have the capability to love. I think that this is something they should learn in schools, to learn how to overcome their fears and to learn how to truly communicate. We need to knock down the prejudices and barriers, because when we talk about safety, safety is really just overcoming fear through the feeling of community. In this project for life, we need to rediscover the relationship of mankind with nature, with God, with our fellow man. I think from there we can begin to create a new future for humanity."

• • •

Aung San Suu Kyi spoke softly about the means for dispelling the cause of fear, which she saw as insecurity, "The first step is confidence building. If the two sides can start having confidence in the other's goodwill, then you can carry on from there, then I think they will be much more honest and not just talk about what they hate, but what they fear. Hate and fear are the opposite sides of the same coin. It's the same thing. You don't hate unless you fear, basically." Máiread spoke again, emphatically, declaring to those caught in the cycle of fear and hatred, "Don't be afraid! Give up your fear." She went on to explain:

"When I started to work for peace, I was afraid," she continued, "but fear blocks us from doing things and believing in ourselves and believing in each other. We're all born to love and be loved. We all need each other. Don't be afraid to go out and be happy and show affection and show love and forgive and ask forgiveness, because we all make mistakes.

"You know that Gandhi was afraid? He was afraid of snakes and growing up in India must have been awful — being afraid of snakes. Someone said to him to keep saying, "Rama, rama" — become aware of the presence of God. Know that you are created in the image of God and that you are loved and capable of loving and you lose all of your fear. You become able to love.

"I would say to young people today, don't be afraid of anything. Lose your fear and give it away — throw it away and start loving. Love everybody and don't let flags and religions get in the way of looking somebody in the eye and seeing the beauty of the human person. When the chips are down, people can come up and do pretty wonderful things. Yet we are capable of great evil. This is for *each* of us. We are all capable of murder — if those things that we love are threatened, but we are also capable of love and doing the greatest things. We need nonviolence because we are capable of great evil and we have nonviolence which makes us capable of great good."

· · ·

Máiread had eloquently voiced what was on the heart of many, the relationship between ignorance, fear and hatred, but also of the remarkable moral power of love. Oscar Arias brought the conversation back to the real issues of our day by speaking of his experience in Central America in relation to this power:

"I believe that moral power is as important, if not more so, than economic and military might. Many of the world's most successful nations are not considered great powers. If we have learned anything in our search for peace and democracy, it is that military power can be confronted with the moral force of those who believe that negotiation and dialogue are the most valuable means to resolve conflicts. It was this moral force which led us to orient Central America towards the course of peace at a time when the great powers attempted to promote a regional war."

Máiread Corrigan Maguire

Gratitude for Mother Earth

We had come full cycle. In seeking the root causes of conflict and suffering, the Nobel Laureates had moved past the more obvious economic and political factors to those that lay behind them. They seemed to agree that ignorance led many to grasp for quick solutions to the problem of poverty which only impoverished others. Ignorance likewise led to ethnic and religious misunderstanding and violence, and to the exploitation of the Earth's resources without a long-term strategy of sustainability. Wangari Maathai closed the morning session. When she spoke I had the feeling that her words sounded out not only on behalf of humanity as a call for good governance, but that she also spoke for what the indigenous traditions have always called Mother Earth.

"Well, from my perspective, my very clear understanding (including an observation from where I live in Kenya and in that region of Africa), it has become very clear to me that many of the conflicts that we have on this planet are due to the fact that we are competing for the limited resources that are available and we are not willing to share them equitably, we are not willing to manage them responsibly.

"I was born in Nyeri, and as I was growing up I was always working with my mother on the land, barefeet, working with my little hands. So the soil is very close to me and I know that the soil is a wonderful resource — that without the soil, we would not have other resources such as wildlife, such as food, such as forests, trees — all the wonderful things such as fresh air. All of the wonderful things that we take for granted and which ensure that we survive are there because we have the soil and we have this system which seems to thrive from the soil, and it is from the soil that even we come from. That's why the religious leaders remind us that we are dust and into dust we will return because we are indeed part of the soil. It's almost automatic for me to want to feel the soil and want to remind myself of the wonders that we have on this planet and to understand that all these systems — the waters, the forests, the soil, the wildlife — they're all interconnected and so are we, and to appreciate that we, the human species, are part of this system — we are not apart, we are part of that system. I like to remind our human species (and this sometimes comes as a surprise to other people) that when you think about it, many other species including plants and animals can live very comfortably without us, but we cannot live without them. So we need to be very grateful, we need to be very appreciative of the other species and we need to give them an opportunity to be, to live whether we are using them or not, whether we love them or not, whether they look beautiful or not. That's none of our business. They have a space in the system and indeed, they should be. Because indeed, we never know sometimes the role that those creatures and those species play in our own survival.

"I want to mention here a word that I learned in Japan when I was there. I learned that they have a word called *mottainai*, and in that word, they also incorporate the concept of 'be grateful for what you get from Mother Earth — receive with gratitude, do not waste and remember that future generations will use the same resources' . . . So we need to think about this, just like those who lived before us thought about us. When you think they handed over to us a beautiful planet, we ought to do the same to the future generations. Now that concept of *mottainai* is a beautiful concept that I'm really also sharing with other parts of the world especially because it comes from a society that is so rich, it can afford to buy anything — but that it is questioning itself and reminding itself that it's important to not overuse, to recycle, to reuse, to be grateful, and that's very important and that's something those of us in developing countries can also learn. Because sometimes we also take for granted what we have from nature, and we're not so grateful and we're not so appreciative of what we receive from nature and what we give back to nature to make sure that she can support the future just like she is supporting us right now."

In Wangai Maathai's words I heard an unconventional vision, one that saw the Earth with all its resources — mineral, plant, animal, and human — as one interconnected eco-system. Likewise the present was inseparable from the past and the future, and we were responsible for all of it. She articulated a view that I knew resonated with many of those in the room, and I was anxious to develop it further, but we had done enough work for one morning. So with an expression of gratitude to all, I adjourned the session for lunch. The gathering broke up into groups of twos and threes and, amid much animated conversation, gradually disappeared down the hall.

Wangari Maathai, Shirin Ebadi and Jody Williams

14

The Wellsprings of Social Renewal and Healing

The conversations over the lunch break had invigorated everyone. I wanted to move the focus of our attention away from the root causes of conflict and suffering to the means of reducing conflict and alleviating suffering. After the Nobels were back in their chairs, I opened immediately with the question, "If ignorance is central to suffering, what can we do about it? Do you see ways of addressing the fundamental ills of our time at the same level from which they arise and not merely treat the symptoms?" José Ramos-Horta from East Timor spoke up to suggest one direction for the group's consideration.

"There are a number of root causes of some of the conflicts that we have. One is ignorance. If you have people who are uneducated, they are more vulnerable to manipulation, brainwashing and instigation by demagogues, whether political demagogues or irresponsible religious demagogues. One answer is to provide better education — more access to the internet, more access to news, to books from the most diverse sources, to teach respect and tolerance for each other so that you defeat the evils of the demagogues, whoever they are."

Levels of education

Oscar Arias spoke next, building on the theme of education begun by José Ramos-Horta, but taking it considerably further. "Education began the day you were born; you learned to breathe to survive and to cry when you wanted food or attention. You then entered grammar school and learned to read and write and socialize with your peers. And as you enter into what students so often call, 'the real world,' you will ingress in the University of Life and learn more than you ever imagined possible, for education is an ongoing and everlasting process that will continue to bring you new insights every day of your life.

"If a nation is to avoid intolerance and bask in the glow of its diversity, it needs wise and strong leaders, leaders with a vision and strength to inspire their fellow citizens to accept and respect one another. In a world often torn by difference, few people embody the personal characteristics needed to lead in this manner: concern for others, selflessness, strength, and undying optimism. Education for the twenty-first century must therefore not only teach the skills and knowledge necessary to lead, but also shape the attitudes and beliefs essential to ensure the benevolent application of that knowledge."

In his remarks Oscar Arias had led us far beyond education as information transfer and the development of skills. No, Arias saw education as involving a transformation of the individual that begins on the day of our birth and proceeds throughout life. Formal education likewise shapes us in a profound and deep way, such that "attitudes and beliefs" are formed in order to ensure that human knowledge is used for the greatest benefit of all. The way in which one should address ignorance had, with Arias's comments, shifted to a more fundamental level, one I found very exciting. Adolfo Pérez Esquivel from Argentina was the next to speak, and he took up Arias's direction fully.

"When one speaks of disarming consciousness," a theme close to Adolfo's heart, "of ridding consciousness of violence, it has to start from childhood up to adulthood. Educators would say that in order to educate one child we need an entire community. It's a cultural change. It's a change of thought and attitudes. In order for this to happen we need to work on the means of communication and on forms of education which present us with models of violence. . . . When we seek change in order to disarm 'armed consciousness,' we need to revise all educational contents. For example, instead of validating war heroes or soldiers or even individuals, we should be developing a culture of solidarity. If we don't manage to disarm our 'armed consciousness' we shall only make more profound the violence in which humanity lives today."

Adolfo Pérez Esquivel's strong emphasis on the internal correlate to outer violence was certainly entirely correct — the laws of a society only hold if they reflect the values held personally by the large majority of its citizens. I was reminded of Ralph Waldo Emerson's line, "It is really a thought that built this portentous war establishment, and a thought shall also melt it away. Every nation and every man instantly surround themselves with a material apparatus which exactly corresponds to their moral state, or their state of thought." That is to say, if inwardly we are preoccupied by violence, then that habit of consciousness will eventually find its outer expression in weaponry and acts of violence. Education becomes then a means of freeing the mind from the tyranny of mental violence, in this way "disarming consciousness" and so disarming the world.

The Dalai Lama, seated cross-legged on his broad chair, spoke in his deep, firm voice, concerning the possibility of change, both of the individual and of society. "There is always the possibility for things to change and to change for the better — changes full of human value; I think that is our goal. We have the opportunity, particularly the young people, who are carrying the responsibility for a good future in the long term." He turned to the several young guests in the room and spoke to them directly. "You are the seed to develop a prosperous, friendly, harmonious, peaceful world. So much depends on you. Education is important, but education alone is not sufficient. Education of the brain and development of the good heart —

these must go together. Good heart gives you courage, gives you the confidence and the determination. These are the prime movers for a better future. And the brain, it is like an instrument, it can solve all our problems. So with a good instrument used by a good heart, then there is real hope, there is a real good future. So you see, much depends on our own shoulders, on our own hands. Let us try to achieve that kind of happy world. Yes, definitely, there is good hope, there is good potential. It is very important to have full confidence and determination to lead that kind of world."

The theme of education in its broadest sense could have occupied us for the remainder of the session. Surely, any attempt to address the fundamental problem of ignorance must include the creation of educational initiatives that work at many levels. The proper development of future generations will require more than technical competencies, as important as these are. Clearly, the Nobel Laureates believed that not only must one offer a global education that informs youth about the diverse people with whom they will need to live, but we must attend to the heart as well.

True Security

"As several of you emphasized this morning," I began, "fear is one of the psychological forces that distorts our perceptions of each other and drives much that takes place on the world stage. How might we address this fear which is a root cause of conflict?" Adolfo had heard my question, but his attention was on Máiread. The two of them were old friends. Máiread had supported Adolfo in his times of crisis in Argentina, and nominated him for the Nobel Peace Prize. In answering my question Adolfo spoke from the heart concerning human security, and his words were directed to Máiread, who responded in kind.

"Well, Máiread, I am very pleased to see you again. In preparation for this 10th Anniversary celebration for PeaceJam, one of the things I would like to talk about is the question of human security, as opposed to military security. We are all working together to construct new possibilities for life in the future, and so I think it is very appropriate to discuss the question of the safety of mankind. In my opinion, I feel that the safety of mankind begins in the community. We are not human beings alone; we are human beings socially, spiritually, politically and economically, in concert with each other. I believe that it is through the community, the community of the family, the community of our villages, of our religious beliefs — this is what enables us to have security and to grow as persons. We cannot stay in the mind-set of 'individualism.'"

Máiread responded with an open heart. "It is lovely to see you again, Adolfo. It is good to be together again. And I agree with you that security really starts within the community, within the family. It is how we build solidarity. We are social animals, we all need each other; we need each other for that sense of love, that sense of support, that sense of belonging. We need roots in community, and when people are uprooted, it can be very frightening for them and very dangerous. Unfortunately, we seem to operate in the world today on a top down model, and we have at the top militarism and political institutions, and people in communities can feel powerless, that they have no control over their lives. They are marginalized from the decision-making at the top, and all the solutions seem to be imposed on them from the top, from the government, top down. And in a sense, if we are to create real live democracies, to create real living democracies, we must build them from the bottom up, build from the villages, build from the communities and empower people both politically and economically in the communities in which they live. I always say that you can't build a house from the top down. You have to really build profoundly strong foundations for a happy, secure society. And that happens in the communities, empowering people economically and politically to have decision-making power over their lives, so that wisdom can rise up to the top. The 'beloved community,' which Martin Luther King spoke about, starts in the home and the villages, at a local level."

Adolfo nodded appreciatively and went on. "Yes it does. What do you think about the safety of mankind? Because when one talks about safety, we talk about the army, the police, of repression, to make more rules, to build more weapons, and to lock ourselves in our homes. I believe that this generates more insecurity than security. It seems to me that the biggest dangers facing humanity in our lifetime come from these massive scientific technological advancements, which have stripped from us our belonging in community."

"Indeed," replied Máiread.

"One of the great challenges for humanity," added Adolfo, "is that we all come from such different experiences. You come from Northern Ireland and I come from the south of Latin America, from Argentina. Yet we have both had experiences of violence, of death, of terror and social injustice. The important issue is how to communicate to youth the hope for a new and different world. How can we teach youth to look at life in a different way — with hope, with values and with human dignity? I think that is a big challenge. One of the things I would like to say to the youth who are listening and watching us is that you visited me in Argentina when our country was suffering under a brutal military dictatorship, and you did it with lots of courage in order to support me. You visited me after I was 'disappeared,' held and tortured for 15 months, and then sequestered under house arrest." The room had become very still; all could feel the emotional intensity of the exchange between these two friends, part of a "beloved community."

"Yes, I remember that well, for it was a powerful experience for me," Máiread replied.

"That was when you nominated me for the Nobel Peace Prize. And once I was released from house arrest, I finally was free to visit you in Northern Ireland. There was an extraordinary exchange between us, even though we do not speak the same language, because violence everywhere has the same face. In reality, this story is a story of hope, and of the ways in which we can give hope and strength to each other." His last words hung in the air: "the ways in which we can give hope and strength to each other." Here was the communal source of human security. It lay in what we give each other, not in what we take for ourselves. And we can always offer each other hope and strength.

Aung San Suu Kyi had been listening keenly, and when Adolfo finished she said, "It is perfectly natural that all people should wish for a secure refuge. It is unfortunate that in spite of strong evidence to the contrary, so many still act as though security would be guaranteed if they fortified themselves with an abundance of material possessions. The greatest threats to global security today come not from the economic deficiencies of the poorest nations but from religious, racial (or tribal) and political dissensions raging in those regions where principles and practices which could reconcile the diverse instincts and aspirations of mankind have been ignored, repressed or distorted. Man-made disasters are made by dominant individuals and cliques which refuse to move beyond the autistic confines of partisan interest. An eminent development economist has observed that the best defense against famine is an accountable government. It makes little political or economic sense to give aid without trying to address the circumstances that render aid ineffectual. No amount of material goods and technological know-how will compensate for human irresponsibility and viciousness."

Jody Williams wished to reinforce what others had said and return us to the root causes of conflict and the proper response to fear. "Well, to me, they all fall under the human security rubric. Instead of seeing each country as a little defended state with national security requirements that make me have more weapons to make my own country safe, we have to think in terms of human security. If we meet the basic needs of everyone on the planet (more or less), if we address the basic environmental threats of the planet, we're increasing security for everybody. That's a huge psychological shift, particularly for governments and militaries, but I think it's one of the consequences of the globalized world. You really have to understand what changed security in this changed world is. I think if we can deal with human security, the environment and ignorance, we might have a chance at not being the agents of our own extinction. That's one of my hopes."

Oscar Arias summed up the conversation well in a clear and simple way. "We must change our way of thinking about security, prosperity, and military prowess. No nation should be secure but in liberty, rich but in compassion, nor strong but in the sense that other nations share equal fortitude. If we make these ideas our guiding principles, they will ultimately be our saving grace."

Good Governance

The contributions by Jody and Aung San Suu Kyi had shifted the focus of the conversation from the true basis of human security to the essential role that governments play in either undermining or supporting the humane conduct of societies. Several of the Nobels had something to say on this matter. Oscar Arias had the floor, and as the newly re-elected President of Costa Rica he had definite opinions concerning the crucial role of governments and the political process.

"Well, I think, yes, politics needs to be changed," began Oscar Arias. "I think that after September 11th the struggle against terrorism is accepted because terrorism is a common enemy for all of humanity. But it's not the only enemy, it's not the only evil that we are going to have to confront. We have poverty, we have illiteracy, we have diseases, we have the degradation of the environment. We have so many things which we are not overcoming, because we have not dedicated sufficient resources to eradicate those evils; I would add the cynicism of double discourse — we proclaim freedom while restricting individual liberty. We proclaim democracy, and when necessary we defend autocracies — because they still exist — if they are our friends or if they supply our oil. We speak of saving the planet and we poison the air, poison the water of the rivers, the water of the seas and we fell the trees of the forests. Finally we speak of peace and we make war. As such, for the youth, for the new generations, this double speak is evidence of the hypocrisy of the political class, the cynicism of this political class, the lack of transparency and sincerity between discourse and action, between what is preached and what is done.

• • •

"I think it's very difficult for this change to occur if we don't change our values, if we don't change our ethics entering the 21st century. I repeat, if one has wrongheaded values, priorities will be amiss and actions will also be amiss. To give you one example, it's incomprehensible that when there is no Cold War, when we only have one super economic and military power, the world still wastes nearly a trillion dollars on weapons and soldiers without being able to fulfill the most basic needs of human beings. The fact that the wealthy world wastes more than 250 billion dollars on agricultural subsidies to protect 11 million agriculturalists in Europe, Japan and North America instead of eliminating agricultural protectionism, instead of buying that food where it is produced in much cheaper fashion and as such helping the farmers of the destitute world in Africa, in Asia, and in Latin America. It appears to me, as we have seen in all the PeaceJam reunions, what the children of the world hope to see are more colleges, more schools, more health-clinics, sport complexes, more anti-drug money; money against vices and in favor of more spending in culture, sports, in strengthening the youth with a better education, in giving them computers in rural schools of the poor world, and eventually giving them access to the internet instead of financing armies and acquiring weapons that, possibly, not only impoverish more and more those people, but also are used at any moment to reprimand its own people or even make war. As long as these priorities don't change, certainly it is difficult to be an optimist as we begin the 21st century. Furthermore, everyone was hoping for the Cold War to end and that we would be able to enjoy the dividends of peace, something which hasn't happened, and we were hoping that we would begin the 21st century with the optimism and confidence that this would be the century of peace. Nevertheless, we began it with an invasion of Afghanistan, with an invasion of Iraq and threats that at any moment there can be new invasions violating international rights with a new concept, a new theory, of 'preventive war'; which really is a threat to peace in the world. For this reason, there will be a lot of work and we have to work, you, us in the public sphere, in the political sphere, religions, the leaders of the private sector, trade-union leaders, business managers, teachers, university professors, and also the responsi-

Oscar Arias

bility of human beings as fathers and mothers to try to create new values for the younger generations."

Arias' powerful words were a stinging indictment of the misguided priorities and policies of many governments around the world. They prompted Betty Williams to express her disappointment in the current conduct of international foreign policy, and also to point to the role of nonviolent opposition.

"First of all," remarked Betty, "we have to hold governments responsible for what they do, and that's number one. I can remember the days when the world looked at the United States — the Constitution of the United States of America was something that every country wanted. In fact, my own country, Ireland, and the Constitution of the Republic of Ireland was based very much on the Constitution of the United States. I think that the biggest threat to peace in our world is the fact that militarism rules the day and we have to get to the stage where pacifism rules the day. To be a pacifist doesn't mean that you have to be nonviolent, and when I say that, I mean I have a very violent tongue when it's necessary. Violence comes in all forms, whether it be from a gun or a tongue. The gun destroys and I hope what I say provokes thought because I always think dissension provokes thought. It's very hard to keep yourself stabilized and say to yourself, 'I've got to be stronger,' because every blow that is thrown at nonviolence, we have to be able to take it on the chin and prove that nonviolence is the weapon of the strong." Máiread joined in, pointing to the tragic consequences when governments fail their people by violating their civil rights, disrespecting their dignity, and ignoring their voice. Violence is the outcome.

"The whole question of human rights is so important," said Máiread. "If you take the situation we experienced in Northern Ireland, when the government removed basic civil liberties, and where young people felt that living in communities, that they were not respected and their rights were not respected. We're all human, and every human being, I believe, has a sense of what is just and what is not just. If we live with injustice and see no redress to this injustice, no channels of communication, no channels by which these things get right, then that anger can grow, that frustration can grow — it can turn into despair, and it can turn into violence. We have seen this in Northern Ireland with bombs, we have seen it in suicide bombings in Palestine — not because young Palestinians are any different from us, but because the repression on the Palestinian people has been too long and too painful. We're seeing it now in Iraq. Why? Not because young Muslims are any different, but because their country has been invaded and occupied; their resources are being usurped. Whenever you perpetrate these gross injustices on people, it's only logical there's going to be a big fight of violence. So we need to uphold human rights, uphold international laws and create justice and equality in society if we really want to see a difference for peace."

Máiread's call for the respect of persons, for human rights and international law, was something everyone in the room had fought for throughout their lives. As I looked around the room, I recalled how each of them had been the victim of oppression, how their human rights had been violated. The realities about which Máiread had spoken were no textbook abstractions, but the lived experience of all those in the room. And behind each of the Nobels I sensed thousands and millions of others whose human rights had been violated. Thousands were in prisons today, many were being tortured, and countless numbers had died. Today we remembered them, and spoke out on their behalf. They were and are part of our beloved community.

"How to make governments understand?" sighed Adolfo Pérez Esquivel. "How do we make politicians understand, because they are the ones who make the decisions? How do we proceed now that democracies and values are in crisis? How do we react when nations or peoples fight with each other, kill one another, violate one another, massacre each other?" Looking at Máiread once again, Adolfo said, "We were both in Iraq and we could see the suffering of that country. Today we see the fighting, the terror and destruction. We see how lies are being used to cover up the truth. What do you think about this? This is something that youth see every day and I think that the challenge is finding the truth, to stand up for human rights and human dignity. I think we need the capability of resistance, a resistance that is social, political and cultural. How do we change this culture of death to a culture of life? I think it is a question that we all face."

Máiread responded with strength and even joy. "I do think the best way for young people to gain confidence in themselves — because we are all afraid, and we all lack confidence — the best way to do that is to reach out to someone else and work together on a project, or help someone else in some way. Then you rise out of your own sense of ego and you are serving people around you. The PeaceJam program, by helping young people get involved, to pursue their own projects and ideas, is very, very empowering. We can actually empower each other. We are not solitary people; we empower each other. Working together, going out and doing something that makes the world more beautiful, this is peace work. Singing, dancing, art, anything that creates beauty in life is peace work. We all say, 'I can do that!'"

The empowerment that comes from working with others, from solidarity around a just cause, was well-known to everyone present. Rigoberta Menchú Tum and Shirin Ebadi spoke on behalf of those who historically have not been in the seats of power and government: indigenous people and women.

"Racism is pathological in society," said Rigoberta. "It is a psychological disease, it is a disease of those who practice it. But just the same as any other addiction, the racists are going to say that they are not racists. And to convince them that this is a negative attitude will be an intense battle. And it is a fight for black people, Latin Americans, indigenous people, women — it is a fight for millions. So then, why don't we fight against it?"

Rigoberta paused pensively for a moment before continuing. "I think these inequalities can be solved if we can rescue spirituality. Spirituality puts you face to face with life with a great deal of humility, and all your pains and successes are gratifying because you are someone who spends very little time on this earth, and you need to live it and be an example. But also, spirituality is a personal attitude of human beings, and that's the reason why women need to spend a lot of time with their daughters and sons. If women teach their children the value of water, the value of air, the value of the sun, the moon, the light we all need, surely those children will think in a holistic way about the future. But this is not only idealistic — I think this is already happening. In many places in the world where there are people who are once again harkening to their ancestral values, their dignity, and their identity and that is why they feel happy. They have self-esteem. And if a group of people has self-esteem, it radiates joy to others.

"My biggest desire is to be a deep part of the millenary Mayan culture. The Mayans are great grandparents, transparent grandparents, and wise grandparents. And that wisdom is not dead. It is within us. It is in the rocks, in the volcanoes, in the rivers and in the earth."

Shirin Ebadi chimed in, saying, "I see the entire world as a theater. The women were always behind the scene, but they were always important and were never recognized. Over time they found confidence, and now they are on the stage. The first woman who appeared on the stage also enabled all other women to get the courage to come on stage, and therefore have confidence. And as more women appear in the theater, they have to raise the screen so more women appear on the stage. And this is the obligation of women who are on the stage, to assure that other women have equal access and equal right to participate in their stage, and we start that from here today."

Choosing Light

Wangari Maathai, one of the first women on the stage of Kenya in some important ways, then spoke. She gathered together the threads of the afternoon's conversation.

"There are many wars being fought all over the world. If you look at them from the perspective of human security, it is what Jody and Shirin have said. If we truly wanted to accept that we are human beings as a species, and that we wanted to survive, and that we wanted to do to others what we would like others to do to us, and we promoted justice, equity in this world, then we would have less conflict. But as long as there are people who want more, who want to control, then man will always find it easy to fight. We all remember the words of Mahatma Gandhi — 'There is enough in the world for every man's need, but not for every man's greed.' Now we are challenged to raise our consciousness towards that goal, towards that dream, towards that awareness."

Jody Williams responded, "I would like to compliment what my sister Laureate Wangari just said about choice. Wangari was saying, we as human beings need to choose a different way. I think part of that choice is recognizing that violence is not some intrinsic quality necessarily of the human being. Violence is a choice. Human beings are making violent choices which are affecting all of us on this fragile planet. And we need to say no to violence as a choice to resolve our common problems on this very fragile planet or we are next."

The final words of the afternoon session were those of Aung San Suu Kyi. She fixed her steady inner gaze not only on the great inequities of our time, but also on the small but unmistakable beacons of light that shine through the dark.

"In the most troubled areas of the world," she started slowly, "reserves of tolerance and compassion disappear, security becomes non-existent and creature comforts are reduced to a minimum — but stockpiles of weapons abound. As a system of values this is totally mad. By the time it is accepted that the only way out of an impasse of hate, bloodshed and social and economic chaos created by men is for those men to get together to find a peaceful solution through dialogue and compromise, it is usually no longer easy to restore sanity. Those who have been conditioned by systems which make a mockery of the law by legalizing injustices, and which attack the very foundations of harmony by perpetuating social, political and economic imbalances, cannot adjust quickly — if at all — to the concept of a fair settlement which places general well-being and justice above partisan advantage.

"During the Cold War the iniquities of ruthless governments and armed groups were condoned for ideological reasons. The results have been far from happy," said Aung San Suu Kyi with sorrow. "Although there is greater emphasis on justice and human rights today, there are still ardent advocates in favor of giving priority to political and economic expediency — increasingly the latter. It is the old argument: achieve economic success and all else will follow. But even long-affluent countries are plagued by formidable social ills which have provoked deep anxieties about the future. And newly rich nations appear to be spending a significant portion of their wealth on arms and armies. Clearly there is no inherent link between greater prosperity and greater security and peace — or even the expectation of greater peace. Both prosperity and peace are necessary for the happiness of mankind, the one to alleviate suffering, the other to promote tranquility. Only policies that place equal importance on both will make a truly richer world, one in which men can enjoy *chantha* [or well-being] of the body and of the mind. The drive for economic progress needs to be tempered with an awareness of the dangers of greed and selfishness which so easily lead to narrowness and inhumanity. If peoples and nations cultivate a generous spirit which welcomes the happiness of others as an enhancement of the happiness of the self, many seemingly insoluble problems would prove less intractable.

"It is the love of ordinary people, in Burma, in Japan or anywhere else in the world, for justice and peace and freedom that is our surest defense against the forces of unreason and extremism that turn innocent songs into threatening war-chants."

Silence followed Aung San Suu Kyi's words, but after a time smiles returned to the faces of all gathered, and each thanked the other for a day well-spent. They warmed to the thought of a good meal and an unscheduled evening with each other, as they drifted down the long hallway lit only by the warm glow of a setting sun.

15

Community and Interconnectedness

I began the second day by referring to an important theme touched on in the previous day's conversation.

"Adolfo spoke yesterday about the importance of community in human security. I would like to turn our attention to this theme in our conversations, but before I do I would like us to consider the opposite of community. Many people, not only the young, feel deeply alone, powerless; they verge on depression and even suicide. You have known them. How can we speak to them? What can we say or do?" Máiread was moved to speak out of one of the most painful experiences of her life.

Powerless and Alone

"The Peace People started because my young sister Anne took four of her children for a walk and three of the children were killed in a clash between the IRA and the army. And another young man, an IRA man, only 19 — was shot through the head, so four young people died that day.

• • •

"My sister recovered slightly. She had two children. In January 1980 she took her own life, took her own life very painfully. It took her a long time to die. She took it because — life was so hard for her that she never got over the death of her children and she left a little note to her family saying forgive me I'm sorry I can't go on.

"It was very hard for her family to...they missed her so much because they loved her so much...So, I would like that those who are alone and depressed go out and talk to a good friend and explain your pain to that friend. The pain one's going through, I know it's very deep, but people *do* care. Find someone who will listen and then, go talk to someone else who is suffering from loneliness.

"I do believe that loneliness is the gravest disease in the world today. We all put on our masks. We pretend we are all doing very well. We keep smiling and...we let on to each other that...we don't have any problems. Life is very, very hard — very painful.

"There's no one that doesn't get heavy crosses throughout life in one way or another. But we have each other to turn to in the hard days. Then the sun comes out again and it's like the seasons. We all come through our winters, but the spring comes and summer comes and it's like that in your life. When you're in your winter go out and find a friend and you'll soon come into your spring and your summer."

Aung San Suu Kyi picked up on the feeling of powerlessness. She seemed unsure to begin with.

"Do the youth of today really feel powerless?" she asked. "It is probably because they have less of a community feeling. You may feel powerless as one alone, but if you're part of a community, I think you would feel less powerless. Perhaps the reason they feel powerless is because they feel apart from the rest of the community — that the generation feels apart from other generations. If they could be made to feel a part of humanity in general — not just part of a generation, an isolated group, they would feel more powerful.

"But is power all that is necessary? Is power all that desirable? That's another question you have to put forth. I've always thought that the best solution for those who feel helpless is for them to help others. I think then they will start feeling less helpless themselves."

The True Friend

Máiread had spoken of the importance of speaking to a friend when burdened by the sorrows of life, when passing through the winter of one's life. So I asked, "What is the role of friendship in the work of peacemaking?" Máiread started off the conversation by referring to the words of the Trappist monk Thomas Merton.

"I take real inspiration from Merton's insight that 'in the end, it is the reality of personal relationships that saves everything.' Merton puts his finger on what is for me one of the 'fruits' of the peace movement. My own life has been greatly enriched by the people whom I have had the privilege to know and work with and call 'friends,' both in the early years of Peace People and today." Some of those friends were sitting in the circle with her that day. The Dalai Lama added his thought to the importance of true friendship and how to cultivate it.

"Everybody wants to have friends and does not want enemies," started the Dalai Lama. "The proper way to create friends is to have a warm heart, not simply money or power. The friend of power and the friend of money are something different: these are not true friends. True friends should be real friends of heart, shouldn't they? I am always telling people that those friends who come around when you have money and power are not truly your friends, but friends of money and power, because as soon as the money and power disappear, those friends are also ready to leave. They are not reliable. Genuine, human friends stand by you whether you are successful or unlucky and always share your sorrow and burdens. The way to make such friends is not by being angry, nor by having good education or intelligence, but by having a good heart."

Aung San Suu Kyi sat very still with a small smile on her lips. She had something to say to the question of friendship, so I gestured to her to begin.

"A doctor once recommended thinking happy thoughts as a most effective remedy for diverse illnesses," she started. "Certainly one of the happiest of thoughts is one's friends; old friends with whom you have shared youthful dreams of an ideal world, new friends with whom you are striving to achieve a realistic version of that ideal. It is comforting to know that friends you have not met for several decades, leading secure lives in countries where their rights are protected by the law, care as much for your welfare now as they did in the days when the Beatles were young and you argued over Dag Hammerskjöld's *Markings*."

Shirin Ebadi interrupted to say concerning her time of imprisonment in Iran that she too had deeply valued the connection to friends. With a touch of humor she explained that because government press releases were issued earlier in America and Asia, she received phone calls from worried friends hours before her arrest. "That day the phone did not stop ringing. For hours I repeated over and over that I was not in prison. Yet."

Archbishop Desmond Tutu laughed, then leaned forward with a twinkle in his eye. "You know, we in South Africa have something we call *ubuntu*. *Ubuntu* — everybody who states the concept makes it too cerebral. It is something that is quite obvious — a person is a person through other persons. I can be human only through relationships with other human beings. Because I wouldn't know how to speak as a human being, I wouldn't know how to think as a human being, I wouldn't know how to talk, I wouldn't know how to be human except through learning it from other human beings.

"Actually, I say that we can be human only together. We can be prosperous only together. We can be free only together. We can be secure, ultimately, only together. And it is in fact this dream that I spoke about earlier, God's dream, that we will realize that we are family. And until we do, we're going to find that all kinds of things go wrong. That at our best, it is when in fact we show that we are connected."

From Isolation to Connection

"From what you have just said," I began, "one of the fundamental misperceptions of modern consciousness may be that of separateness or isolation. While each of us honors the unique gifts and nature of the individual, we seem too weakly aware of our pervasive interconnection to others. We treasure the friendship between two people as an encouraging force of love, yet we seem unconscious of the interconnection of humanity more generally." The Dalai Lama responded to my remarks by describing the profound interdependence of reality and the implications of this fact for our treatment of each other and the environment.

"We are in a New Reality now," stated the Dalai Lama. "We are in a New World, I think, because of the economy, because of the crisis of ecology, the water crisis, all of these things. I think in this New World, everything is heavily interdependent. So now, our approach also should be changed according to that new reality. Sometimes I do feel reality is much changed but that our attitude still tends to be old-fashioned. Sometimes, our approach may be well-intentioned, but it is simply against the reality or does not fit with the new reality; so then our approach becomes unrealistic, or just wishful thinking."

"In today's New World, what does it mean to be moral?" I asked. "What does morality mean?"

"I think the sense of community, the sense of global interdependence in itself can be a moral principle," explained the Dalai Lama. "That means we can no longer have a narrow-minded, self-centered sort of attitude. And respecting others, taking serious consideration of others' welfare is, I think, a fundamental moral principle. It is the concept of love, or the sense of brotherhood and sisterhood. This is the meaning.

"I think in the past, there was a different situation. My hope is the New Reality. The new realities of the world are compelling us to think with a wider perspective. I think in ancient times, they viewed their situation, then, thinking more individually and seeing things in terms of distance between 'we' and 'they.' They said, "OK, our population can remain isolated and self-sufficient, not dependant on others." Under that set of circumstances, the concept of 'we' and 'the enemy' made some sense, and the destruction of the enemy through war was your 'victory.' But now, the current reality is no longer the same. Now, destruction of your neighbor is destruction of your-self. So the basic view of 'we' and 'they,' that we are not dependent on others, that we can be independent, no longer is true. Now, we are compelled to take care of them, because they are also a part of us. There is a new ethic because we realize a new reality. Then, irrespective of whether we are on our own or not, we have to act according to that reality."

I had read about the Dalai Lama's Buddhist understanding of interdependence and so drew him out further on the issue, since it seemed to me that most people were indeed unconsciously and habitually frozen into the Old Reality of isolation and separation. It was important to understand the nature of the New Reality as he saw it.

"The theory of interdependence allows us to develop a wider perspective," the Dalai Lama said. "With wider mind, with less attachment to destructive emotions like anger, and therefore more forgiveness. In today's world, every nation is heavily interdependent, interconnected. Under these circumstances, destroying your enemy—your neighbor — means destroying yourself in the long run. You need your neighbor.

"Now, we're not talking about the complete removal of feelings like anger, attachment, or pride. Just a reduction. Interdependence is important because it is not a mere concept; it can actually help reduce the suffering caused by these destructive emotions.

"We can say the theory of interdependence is an understanding of reality," the Dalai Lama continued. "We understand that our future depends on global well-being."

"How can one develop the consciousness of interdependence as you describe it?" I asked.

"With time, with time," he replied. "Spiritual progress takes time. It's not like switching on a light. More like kindling a fire: it starts from small spark, then becomes bigger and bigger, more light, more light, like that. All mental transformations are like that."

"Since I meditate on or analyze interdependence for many years, now it is already familiar," the Dalai Lama replied. "So therefore, when I look at things, as soon as I remember the truth of interdependence, the picture becomes clearly different. And the sensation comes without much effort—almost automatically."

Here was a powerful and lucid statement of the spiritual development called for in our age. We normally bring a consciousness to the world that analyzes it in terms of parts, and all relationships are derivative from the fragments we think of as primary. His vision of interdependence worked in the opposite direction, emphasizing the holistic, interrelated character of the New Reality, as the Dalai Lama called it. He was advancing something more than a theory; rather it was a way of seeing or being in the world. Learning a theory takes a few days or weeks, but changing who we are and how we see takes years of study and contemplative practice.

Environment Relationships

Rigoberta was anxious to speak. I was not surprised that she wished to extend the theory of interdependence to the Earth. Rigoberta spoke with passion.

"The other great battle for me is to fight for Mother Earth," Rigoberta emphatically stated. "I'm not referring to one parcel, to one farm. I am referring to Mother Earth as the globe, as the planet, as the fountain of life for all peoples. The people do not value Mother Earth. But there is the healing, therein lies life, she's our mother. If we wouldn't have had a mother from whom we were born, surely we would not exist, and Mother Earth is where we were all born. It doesn't matter what color, race, or ethnicity, we are all children of Mother Earth."

The Dalai Lama was clearly in agreement with Rigoberta, saying, "We should extend this attitude to be concerned for our whole environment. As a basic principle, I think it is better to help if you can, and if you cannot help, at least try not to do harm. This is an especially suitable guide when there is so much yet to understand about the complex interrelations of diverse and unique eco-systems. The Earth is our home and our mother. We need to respect and take care of her. This is easy to understand today.

"We need knowledge to care for ourselves, every part of the Earth and the life upon it, and all of the future generations as well. This means that education about the environment is of great importance to everyone. Scientific learning and technological progress are essential for improving the quality of life in the modern world. Still more important is the simple practice of getting to know and better appreciate ourselves and our natural surroundings, whether we are children or adults. If we have a true appreciation for others and resist acting out of ignorance we will take care of the Earth.

"In the biggest sense, environmental education means learning to maintain a balanced way of life. All religions agree that we cannot find lasting inner satisfaction based on selfish desires and acquiring the comforts of material things. Even if we could, there are now so many people that the Earth would not sustain us for long. I think it is much better to practice enjoying simple peace of mind. We can share the Earth and take care of it together, rather than trying to possess it, destroying the beauty of life in the process.

"Ancient cultures that have adapted to their natural surroundings can offer special insights on structuring human societies to exist in balance with the environment. For example, Tibetans are uniquely familiar with life on the Himalayan Plateau. This has evolved into a long history of a civilization that took care not to overwhelm and destroy its fragile ecosystem. Tibetans have long appreciated the presence of wild animals as symbolic of freedom. A deep reverence for nature is apparent in much of Tibetan art and ceremony. Spiritual development thrived despite limited material progress. Just as species may not adapt to relatively sudden environmental changes, human cultures also need to be treated with special care to ensure survival. Therefore, learning about the useful ways of people and preserving their cultural heritage is also a part of learning to care for the environment."

Wangari underscored the movement afoot to work in the ways the Dalai Lama had described. "In the world," she said, "there is a new collective force of people mobilizing around the issue of peace but linking it to the need to protect the environment. But we must assert our collective vision and responsibility to shape that peace not only for our country but also for the whole Earth."

Identity through Community: Ubuntu

"Archbishop, I would like to ask you to come in at this point. When you gave your Nobel acceptance speech you, like so many in this room, pointed to others. You described the Nobel Peace Prize as not yours but theirs, saying,

> This award is for you — Mothers, who sit near railway stations trying to eke out an existence, selling potatoes, selling meali, selling pigs' trotters.

> This award is for you — Fathers, sitting in a single-sex hostel, separated from your children for eleven months of the year.

· · ·

This award is for you — Mothers in the squatter camps, whose shelters are destroyed callously every day and who have to sit on soaking mattresses in the winter rain, holding whimpering babies and whose crime in this country is that you want to be with your husbands.

This award is for you — three and a half million of our people who have been uprooted and dumped as if they were rubbish. The world says we recognize you, we recognize that you are people who love peace.

This award is for you — dear children, who despite receiving a poisonous gruel, designed to make you believe that you are inferior, have said 'there is something that God put into us which will not be manipulated by man, which tells us that we are your children.' This award is for you — and I am proud to accept it on your behalf as you spurn a travesty of an education.

This award is for you, who down the ages have said we seek to change this evil system peacefully. The world recognizes that we are agents of peace, of reconciliation, of love, of justice, of caring, of compassion. I have the great honor of receiving this award on your behalf. It is our prize. It is not Desmond Tutu's prize.

"And I know that others of you have spoken about your co-workers in Argentina, Guatemala and elsewhere as the real winners of the Prize." At this point José Ramos-Horta interrupted to describe his experience in East Timor:

"I would say that the true heroes in my own situation in my country are the unknown people, the common people. When I went back home in '99, I was received like a national hero; thousands and thousands of people came to the streets to welcome me, and wherever I went in the following days and weeks, thousands more were in various places. And I felt embarrassed that I was being received like a national hero, because they were the ones who were there enduring 24 years of occupation without losing hope. And they put so much hope on me and on others. Being the real heroes, they taught me a tremendous lesson in humility. In the face of their greatness, the greatness of giving me the status of being a national hero when they were the real heroes, well, it really humbled me. It's overwhelming."

"Thank you, José That is the kind of story which I know all of you have," I went on, turning back to Desmond Tutu.

"Some say that what we really need to see is a profound shift in global consciousness, in global perception. Do you agree, Archbishop Tutu, and if so, how can we bring such a shift about?"

"Well, this is really what we're trying to say. I mean, the day that we realize that we are actually bound one to another," said Tutu, "that's a shift in consciousness, because at the present time, mostly it is everyone for himself or herself, and the devil take the last in the queue. And as long as we do that, and as long as we think the way to prosperity is by ruthless competition, we've had it. That's how wars happen, because resources are always going to be limited. And if we say resources are going to be the monopoly only of the powerful, we're in trouble. We're in very serious trouble. Whereas if we say, 'Let's begin thinking about sharing'...

"There is a wonderful ethic where you have a properly functioning family. You don't say in the family, 'You get in proportion to what you contribute.' A baby contributes almost nothing, and the oldest member of the family also probably now contributes nothing. But in a good family, those are the ones who get most of the caring, and so in a healthy family, the ethic is, 'From each according to their abilities, to each according to their need.' Now, that might sound utopian, but now and again we offer it on that basis. That is usually when we have disasters, where you don't say, Niger, we are going to give you only what you can afford. No. There's incredible bounty, people just pour out remarkable generosity. Why do we put our generosity into quarantine for most of the time, and bring it out only on special occasions? We're really not going to survive if we think it is going to be survival of the fittest. It won't work, that's the law of the jungle."

As the session drew to a close several in the circle wished to draw these more philosophical reflections back to the concrete realities of globalization. Jody Williams was the first to contribute, and to remark that while a New Reality may be evident to the Dalai Lama and Desmond Tutu, most governments still act out of the old paradigm.

"Oh, I totally agree that the world has changed extremely dramatically, especially since the collapse of the Soviet Union," declared Jody. "That's part of the change, but it's not all of the change. I think that most governments are still reacting to the old world, the way the world was before, that states could actually carry out wars to gain control of resources or to assert their power and that wouldn't have a ripple effect around the world the way it does today. Because of the interconnectedness of the world, because of e-mail, because of the ability to travel so quickly between countries, governments can no longer control all of the factors that are part of an outcome the way that they used to be able to. What governments tried to do in the past (and were pretty successful in doing) was having their population believe that the only things they should worry about, if at all, were domestic issues, and the government would take care of the foreign issues. In today's world, it's so interconnected that I don't see a distinction between what's domestic and what's foreign. And I believe that we all have to accept responsibility for our part in addressing those problems, whether we be an individual, an organization or a government. If we continue to think that alone I can solve the problems, alone I can protect myself, we're going to be living in the stone age and we're not going to be addressing this globalized world and how interconnected the problems are. Therefore the solutions have to be interconnected. Interconnectedness — the world has always seemed that way to me. I obviously understand that with the internet and everything, it's sped up. But I always somehow felt part of the

José Ramos-Horta

whole planet, not just little bitty Vermont where I grew up and then New England and then the United States. I thought I was always part of the whole planet."

José Ramos-Horta spoke next concerning the requirement to address the issue of health, for example, at the international level.

"Some 50 years ago, or even less," said Ramos-Horta, "the wealthy in the West seemed to be immune, and because they believed they were immune, they were also indifferent to the problems in the developing world. Now because of globalization, of interconnectedness brought about by globalization, by the fast movement of people and of goods, they no longer feel so immune from events that happen elsewhere in the globe. And I'm not talking only about terrorism; I'm talking about diseases. We have had in recent times the threat of Avian Flu, of SARS, we have had HIV. Globalization will bring about new epidemics that were eliminated in the West but are still prevalent in many developing countries. They might come to the shores of the Western countries if the Western countries don't do enough to eliminate some of the contagious diseases that are very pervasive in developing countries, like TB, cholera and all of that. So this is the inevitability of globalization; it is negative, but in some ways it's good because it forces humanity to realize that our destinies are intertwined and that we have to work together for the common good of humanity."

"How do you see the situation, Shirin Ebadi?" I asked.

"It is natural that we live in a global era," she replied. "Whatever happens in one place in the world, affects other places as well. On one day, the USA supported the Taliban and Bin Laden and years later some people became victims of terrorism in an explosion in the train in Madrid or on 9/11 in the USA. This is what we mean by how the world has become a small village. If a small corner of it catches fire, it can spread to other parts. We need a consciousness or a change that results in a life of peaceful coexistence. Let me tell you an old story: God was in the seventh heaven and truth was a mirror in God's hands. From the seventh heaven, the mirror fell down to earth and broke into thousands of pieces and each piece fell into a different house and to a different person. Thus truth is with everyone and everyone sees a part of truth. I have as much of the truth as you, and I am just as right as you. If we could expand on this attitude and convince the people, especially the youth, of this truth — that all truth is not with one person or just with us — then we can work together more comfortably."

Our time together was at an end for the second morning. Our conversation had ranged from the deep solitude of the individual to friendship, and the great importance of life within a community. Globalization is knitting us

16

From 9/11
to Nonviolence

We had taken up the root causes of conflict and certain strategies for
dealing with them, but given the many conflicts raging around the world,
how were we to act? What should we do? For the afternoon of the second
day of our imaginary Nobel conversation I, therefore, directed the questions to peace-making in times of violent conflict.

"What," I asked, "can we offer to nations and peoples caught up in violent
conflicts? Governments traditionally respond to attack with political and
military power. The terrorist attack of September 11 has led to the invasions of Afghanistan and Iraq. Oscar has spoken about the efficacy of
'moral power' in the face of conflict, but is this sufficient? What are the
alternatives to military force?" In her response, Shirin Ebadi balanced her
sympathy for those who suffered in the 9/11 attack with hard questions
about the current state of the world.

Post 9/11 Reflections

"Allow me first to express my sorrows for the incident of 9/11 and express my condolences to the survivors," said Shirin Ebadi sincerely. "However, we must pay attention to one issue. Is punishing terrorist action enough to eradicate terrorism from the world? For many years they have been punishing terrorists but have acts of terrorism decreased? No, it has actually survived and unfortunately increased. And this is because the struggle against terrorism must go to its roots. We must know where terrorism springs from and dry it from its roots. The roots of terrorism are in prejudice and ignorance. Prejudice derives from ignorance. People who have little consciousness, people who only know their own culture, religion and civilization, are prejudiced, and therefore do not have any knowledge of other peoples' cultures and religions. Therefore familiarity with other religions and cultures can eradicate prejudice.

"Another root of terrorism is injustice. When there is injustice to one people and there is no way of receiving justice, and when several generations live under the poverty line and there is no hope for the improvement of their lives, they may forget their sanity because of hopelessness. And thus they may resort to violence. Therefore, let's struggle with the root causes of terrorism. We must get to the roots of terrorism. Punishing terrorists to eradicate terrorism is not enough.

"On the other hand, although the punishment of terrorists is allowed by law, it must be carried out within a certain framework. Under the pretext of fighting terrorism, one must not limit the liberties of a people. The fight against terrorism must be carried out within the limits of the UN charters and resolutions. Further, prisons like Guantanamo or Abu Ghraib are causes for shame and hopelessness. Why should such things happen? Therefore, perhaps we are going the wrong way. If we had fought terrorism in the last 40 or 50 years in a way that would have addressed its roots and causes, we would not have witnessed such sad incidents."

"I am saddened," added Archbishop Desmond Tutu, "by the fact that we have been seeing a spirited erosion of rights. I can't believe it is true. I keep having to pinch myself — could it really be true in the only superpower in the world, the United States, and one of the leading countries that taught us democracy, Britain — this can't be true. They actually use the same justification for detention without trial that was used by the apartheid regime. It's unbelievable! And we say, 'Is this what evolution means?' That we come to the point where we say, 'The best way to ensure freedom is to restrict freedom'? That's crazy!

"For me, a South African, it has been a frightening *déjà vu*. That is the way we were in South Africa, that is one of the things I'm so fearful for. Because people are frightened and insecure, they look for Big Brother — 'I will protect you' — and Big Brother says, 'I need to have special powers.' I hope that we would realize that we cannot win the war against terror as long as there are conditions in the world — conditions of poverty, of disease or of ignorance, that drive people to become desperate."

Clearly, the sentiment around the circle was one of great concern. Rigoberta Menchú Tum also wished to be heard on the issue.

"I think the results of September 11TH are very negative results for humanity," commented Rigoberta. "Decisions were made that were honestly infuriating, especially the increase in supposed security and the war in Iraq. The war in Iraq is endless. Simply put, it is another tragedy. Correct decisions were not made."

Jody Williams picked up the thread saying, "I, like many people, hoped after September 11TH when the world came together in concern, sympathy and solidarity with the people of the United States, this country would actually assess what happened, look at the problems in the world and show a different kind of leadership. When you say that, people seem to think that you mean they shouldn't do anything to deal with terrorism.

"Showing a different kind of leadership does not mean that you do not address the issues of terrorism; it does not mean that you don't use force to go after terrorists, just the way police use force to go after lawbreakers. But to respond in a totally predictable fashion — finding an enemy to attack, creating a war of choice in Iraq that now has put us in a situation where I honestly don't know what the answer is. I don't know how this country and the other countries that are supporting the U.S. in that absurd war of choice — how do you get out of that mess in a sane way at this point?

"They have created exactly the situation they didn't want when they created this war. They've created an environment where terrorism can flourish. They've created a focal point for hatred against the policies of the United States. Their policies have produced the opposite of what they said invading Iraq would do. Now they're there, the country is increasingly breaking down (perhaps on the verge of civil war, who knows?), and how do they withdraw at this point without doing exactly what they don't want to do, which is look like they can be forced out of a military situation by their own stupidity? I think it's remarkable.

"I wonder how, with a straight face, this country can lecture anyone on human rights issues after everything we've seen in Abu Ghraib, of course, and Guantanamo, and yet they still try. The hypocrisy is mind-boggling, and maybe many of the people of the U.S. will swallow it, but the world doesn't. The world is not ignorant. The world sees what the U.S. is doing, hears what it says, sees a disconnect between words and action, and makes a judgment that they're hypocrites. Hypocrites don't play well in the world."

Adolfo Pérez Esquivel gave his views in very strong terms.

"September 11TH provoked changes in the United States and in its politics," remarked Adolfo. "This has been very dangerous for the rest of the world because it speaks of 'terrorism' but it doesn't speak of other terrorisms. There is no cause without effect, it's a permanent relationship.

"Therefore, what has changed? More children continue to die of starvation because more money is being invested in weapons when the military budget increased enormously. In this sense I think there have been changes for the worst."

In equally strong terms, Máiread Corrigan Maguire expressed her dismay. "I believe that we are moving in the wrong direction," said Máiread, "and I think particularly the foreign policies of the United States and the U.K. are the wrong policies. It was absolutely dreadful what happened on 9/11, and the whole sympathy of the world was with the American people. But the reaction to it of the attack on Afghanistan, war and invasion of Iraq, all the things that flowed from this were just totally the wrong way.

"We also have some things to teach out of our very sad experience of 30 years of violent actively political conflict in Northern Ireland. We tried to solve these problems through militarism and through paramilitarism and through the government removing many of our basic civil liberties, and all these things don't solve the problem, they were adding fuel to the anger and the frustration. We had a backlash there, with paramilitary insurgency groups, and really it was only when people began to say, 'these human problems, political problems can only be solved through dialogue, through negotiation, through beginning to tackle what is causing the pain of the people in the first place,' and that's a long, slow process. There are no quick solutions to the problems the human family is now faced with. So, I think that Northern Ireland is only a model of what we're going to see more and more around the world; an inability for us to deal with our political problems without exploding into violence. That's why we need to learn nonviolence."

Nonviolence or Non-existence

I took Máiread's remarks as an opportunity to shift the conversation from the disturbing and tragic consequences of 9/11 to the theme of nonviolence.

"If not a military response to attack or conflict, then what? Máiread has suggested that nonviolence in the proper response, but critics will reject it as naïve," I said. Jody Williams was the first to take up my challenge to speak about the the theme of a nonviolent response to conflict, expressing her frustration with those who saw it as born of weakness, cowardice or naiveté.

"People try to disempower those who believe in nonviolent solutions to global problems by calling it 'utopian,' by making peace sound like love — some wimpy little response to global problems." said Jody. "The 'realists' of the world understand the world is mean and ugly, and if you're going to deal with the mean and ugly problems, you've got to kick ass. And if you're some wimpy peacenik, you just don't understand the reality of ugly people like Osama Bin Laden.

"To me, that's counterintuitive. Our country generally runs on the good-will and desire of citizens to be good citizens and to obey the law. There are evil people in the country who break the law that go to jail. Osama Bin Laden is a person who grossly broke the law, and should be taken away. But does that mean you want a war? Does that mean you create a war on terror? Does that mean that you always respond with violence and war to prove that you're a manly man and that real MEN understand that you've got to kick butt in order to prevail?

"Every time somebody says that to me, I give them the example of Aung San Suu Kyi, a woman who has suffered how many years of house arrests because she refuses a violent response to the military dictatorship. That's bravery."

"Can you beat it?" Archbishop Tutu asked incredulously. "The military junta are armed to the teeth and they are scared of a little woman. They run away from Rangoon and hide somewhere in the forest, because she is good and they are scared." But he looked forward to the day when he and the Dalai Lama would be able to attend her inauguration as Burma's president. "Freedom," he concluded, "is unstoppable."

Máiread interjected, "Wisdom means the tough decision to walk the path of nonviolence. That risk of faith will take all your courage."

. . .

Jody went on, "When a country like the United States believes that it needs to control the resources, the power of the world, it denigrates other possible solutions because 'nonviolent solution' implies you sit down, you discuss. So you have to make people who think differently from you seem weak, you denigrate nonviolent solution, you denigrate multi-lateral discussions to resolve problems, you make peace really seem ridiculous and absurd. You conjure up the image that always makes me insane, of the butterflies and birds flying over the rainbow, proving that it's a storybook image of peace.

"There's nothing storybook about peace, it's really hard work all the time. Look at the work of Archbishop Tutu to nonviolently resolve the decades of political violence in South Africa. That was hard work; there was nothing utopian about that. Our work even in the landmine campaign to rid the world of a conventional weapon that kills people all over the world — that was hard work, every day. It's not utopian. You get up and you struggle every day to make a difference in the world. That's not utopian. I wish it were. I wish it were as easy as visualizing world peace. It isn't. It's finding ways to address the things that bother you. People who just want to complain and take no action to resolve the things that bother them, I really have no time for them. I really don't. I don't care to hear that you're concerned about something if you aren't going to tell me what you're doing to make it different. Don't waste my time. There's not enough time to listen to whining."

Jody's tough talk had stirred up a number of the Nobels. Clearly Jody's brand of nonviolent resistance was not limited to soft-spoken protests. Her life had been one of action in Central America and around the world. She, like all the Nobels, was not timid about "speaking truth to power," but at the same time she has little patience with mere complainers. Her mantra was and is "Action does make a difference."

Nonviolence as a Third Way

"You know, in the past, we have always been taught two ways for people to solve their problems," Máiread added. "One has been to fight and the other one has been to run. I think the third way of active nonviolence is much more viable, but we have never been taught nonviolence. I mean, the path of active nonviolence is not even taught in religious seminaries to answer questions about violence in any of our faith traditions. And yet it is in the roots of all our faith traditions, when you take the time to look deeply into it. So, if we begin teaching the techniques of nonviolence, conflict resolution, peer mediation; if we begin to teach real nonviolence, which is, of course, to love your enemy and don't kill them, that is what nonviolence is truly about. And this is much more in harmony with our human spirit. It is natural for us to identify with each other. It is totally unnatural for us to be given a gun and learn to kill and torture each other. You have to be taught that. Human beings are, by nature, good. And I think if we can begin to teach nonviolence in our homes (where we solve our problems through loving each other), if we teach it in our schools, if we teach it in our communities, and if everybody did that around the world, we could very quickly shift from a violent, militaristic, unjust, cruel world to a loving, forgiving, caring world. We would become people who can solve their problems without hurting or killing each other, and that is how it should be. It is just that we've never really learned that this is the way to do it."

Máiread's colleague in the struggle in Northern Ireland, Betty Williams, added her personal experience.

"In Northern Ireland," Betty began, "at one stage in my life I would have picked up a gun, I think, because I saw the injustices being perpetrated on my people. However, the answer is nonviolence. Nonviolence is not a thing that comes easily. You have to learn how to be nonviolent. The toughest thing I've ever done in my live was to be a nonviolent person in Northern Ireland," to which Adolfo replied.

• • •

"The reality is that we have created for ourselves a culture of violence," Adolfo explained. "It teaches us the story of wars, conflicts, and great battles, and the heroes are always heroes of violence. My heart aches when I see our modern means of communication, like the television, where there are sociological studies that say a child from four years of age until they are 18 years old will see more than 40,000 acts of brutality and violence. This is a culture of violence, and we have to try to change this mechanism."

"Yes," Máiread responded, "I agree with you Adolfo, and it is also proven that if children watch over and over again violent images, it desensitizes them to the suffering of others, and they themselves can actually come to see cruelty as almost natural. We are all affected by this."

"And have you noticed how," Adolfo replied, "when something peaceful happens, there is no story. Once there is peace, there is no news. The news media, being a means of communication, does a good job of demonstrating

Betty Williams and the Dalai Lama

the horror of a bomb, and a bomb makes more noise than peace. But peace, peace reconstructs that which has been destroyed, and that is the difference. Once again, I will say that what we need to do is to dismantle the armed consciousness — we need to disarm our minds. If we do not achieve the disarming of the armed consciousness we cannot transform our lives, or the future of humanity. The first thing we must do is to dismantle our own consciousness because we are children of a culture of violence, and our minds have been armed. Each one of us needs to find a way to dismantle our armed consciousness, to begin to recognize ourselves as persons in fellowship with each other, as women and men creating great unity within diversity.

"I think this is the grand challenge," Adolfo continued. "PeaceJam, with all of its programs, is trying to go in that direction. It is trying to generate consciousness for peace, understanding and dialogue; it is a project of life. The mind-set of militarism and individualism is a project of death. It generates conflict, it creates war, it destroys others. This social and structural violence carries death. The challenge is, how can we generate a consciousness like that which is embodied in PeaceJam? I think that peace is the grand revolution that mankind is waiting for."

Once again, a shift in consciousness was called for, one to which not only educators could contribute, but also the media. Our instincts of self-preservation, of "fight-or-flight," need to be met and addressed so that a more compassionate and nonviolent social life might flourish. The Dalai Lama then spoke, adding to the discussion of nonviolence from the Tibetan perspective and about the shift in his own consciousness through a lifetime of meditative practice.

Dalai Lama on Nonviolence

"When I was young," began the Dalai Lama, "I was quite short-tempered. I would sometimes excuse this by saying that it was because my father was short-tempered, as if it was something genetic. But as time passes, I think that now I have almost no hatred towards anybody, including towards those Chinese who are creating misery and suffering for Tibetans. Even towards them, I really do not feel any kind of hatred. I consider hatred to be the ultimate enemy. By 'enemy' I mean the person or factor which directly destroys our interest. Our interest is that which creates happiness.

"We can also speak of the external enemy. For example, in my own case, our Chinese brothers and sisters are destroying Tibetan rights and, in that way, more suffering and anxiety develops. But no matter how forceful this is, it cannot destroy the supreme source of my happiness, which is my calmness of mind. This is something an external enemy cannot destroy. Nothing can destroy this except my own anger.

"Those people whom we know and who create problems for us really provide us with a good opportunity to practice tolerance and patience. Seen from this angle, the enemy is the greatest teacher for our practice."

I pressed the Dalai Lama to see under what circumstances he might depart from nonviolence. Would he use violence in order to free Tibet?

"No," he replied, "I don't think so. In that situation more violence would happen. After all, the most important thing is that China and Tibet have to live side-by-side, whether we like it or not. Therefore, in order to live harmoniously, in a friendly way, and peacefully in the future, the national struggle through nonviolence is very essential."

"Thank you," I said quietly, acknowledging that I was not as far along with my peace of mind as he, but still, as with him, I recognized the change in me over the years. "How do you speak about nonviolence?" I asked the circle. "How do you teach it?" Adolfo had much to say on the issue, and he re-entered the conversation.

Teaching the Gospel of Nonviolence

"Nonviolence is not a very good word for what we are trying to do," Adolfo added. "It makes you think of something negative. Many people think it means passivity. Our friends in Brazil, where the movement is more advanced, call it 'maintained fidelity' or 'steadfastness.' Martin Luther King, Jr., used to call it 'the power of love.' Gandhi didn't like 'nonviolence' either—he preferred *satyagraha* or the 'power of truth.' That is what we mean. If we say 'nonviolence,' it is only because we haven't found a better word."

"Yes," I said. "Gandhi once said that 'in his daily experience every problem lends itself to solution if we are determined to make the law of truth and nonviolence the law of life. For truth and nonviolence are to me, faces of the same coin.'"

"Our work goes on at different levels," explained Adolfo. "First—before any other steps in the liberation process — a human being must become aware that he or she is a person. Our approach is rooted in the gospel. We have to see how to get the gospel into all the areas of human life, all the areas of economics, politics, and culture. We have to see how to keep transforming the situation, how to keep moving toward human liberation on both the spiritual and the social levels. For me the gospel isn't just personal. It needs to be shared.

"We know too that one evil cannot be cured by another. Evils don't cancel each other out. They total up. Christ gives us a commandment, the commandment of love. He also gives us another commandment that is important for us: 'You shall not kill.' And that's it. That's plain. But we find all kinds of excuses. When human beings forget one another, they forget God — and thereby they give up their whole reason for existing. What good is culture, philosophy, or science if men and women become objects instead of subjects? We have always questioned armed liberation movements — for fear today's oppressed will become tomorrow's oppressors. If a human being is an object — just something to be used and thrown away — if every economic, political, or military project comes before persons — then what good are the things of this creation?"

I asked Adolfo, "Where does nonviolence get its power?"

. . .

"First of all, from the active participation of its base—popular resistance. Next, from the application of methods of resisting aggression and injustice. These methods are worked out as a function of the opportunities that arise. There are no ready-made formulas. Formulas only come into being after situations are studied and analyzed. Our methodology is simple: from reflection to action and back to reflection again. We try to size up a situation of conflict, and carefully consider what is motivating the people involved in it. And there is another important point: We try to act in truth. This is what gives our movement its security: the truth—respect for the human person. Respect for the human person generates constancy and steadfastness. And constancy and steadfastness generate attack on evil and the possibility of altering the structures of injustice.

"Many reject violence, but see no other course—no other alternative, no other option to follow. For us there is an alternative: nonviolence. Nonviolence is a challenge, but it is the only option for us as Christians if we wish to effect changes in depth. You see, it's not just a method of fighting. It's not just a mechanism, so that all you'd have to do is put it in gear. It's a manner of being, a way of living. I think we're breaking new ground."

I could not resist inserting another statement of Gandhi's. "Wherever you are confronted with an opponent, we should conquer him with love," said Gandhi.

"I have a couple of very simple ways of explaining the nonviolent method," Adolfo went on to say. "When you play chess or checkers, you and your opponent have to agree to play by the same rules; otherwise the game simply can't take place. Well, in nonviolent combat what we do is just exactly what nice players aren't supposed to do. We refuse to play by one of the rules the system tries to foist on us: that rule that says you have to counter violence with violence. If your opponents can get you to swallow that idea, then they can unleash still greater violence on you. The essential thing in nonviolent combat is for us to render these tactics inoperative by refusing to play by the rules and by imposing our own conditions instead.

"The other example—a very simple one that makes people smile—is that of the battle of the ant and the elephant. True, the elephant is stronger. But the ants ... well, there are more of us. That's why the basic communities are so important; that's why we absolutely have to have basic groups. The basic community has some unique characteristics: It enables each member to find himself or herself as a person. It develops a sense of solidarity, a sense of a community of brothers and sisters.

"Our great hope and encouragement, as we keep organizing the people, is knowing we're getting somewhere. When we look at the people of Latin America today, we see that they have acquired a critical consciousness. They are not the same as they were 15 or 20 years ago. They understand their situation much better, and they demand a concrete response to their problems."

The room was quiet as the Nobels nodded with respect, and the light in the room began to shift as the sun set over the Rocky Mountains. I thanked all of the Nobel Laureates once again for their heartfelt words and simple, clear life wisdom. We all then headed slowly down the hall and into the twilight.

Adolfo Pérez Esquivel

17

Changing Consciousness and the Place of Spirituality

During the second day of our conversation, we had plumbed the tragic depths of war, and we envisioned the possibility of a time when nonviolence was the universally adopted code of conduct. With dozens of conflicts raging around the globe, it is clear that nonviolence is now far from a universal moral precept. On our final day together we returned briefly to the question of a much needed deep transformation or a shift in consciousness within people that could help redirect our future. Within this context several of the Nobel Laureates began to speak about the spiritual dimensions of their work and about the inner resource that their religion or spiritual practice offered them. I began by quoting from a speech of Máiread's in which she called for a change.

"Yesterday we envisioned a nonviolent world," I started to say, "one guided by our moral imagination, a view of ethics that we all largely share. But such a future will require many changes such as true human security based on a more equitable division of the Earth's resources. It will also require a shift of consciousness. We have all spoken about the need for education.

The change you are calling for is profound. Can we spend a little more time together considering that change?"

Call to a Change of Heart

Archbishop Tutu took the floor and asked if he might relate a story that he felt represented a shift in one woman's heart. It was the story of a white woman, Ms. Irene Crouse, who was a wardress in one of South Africa's prisons during the time of apartheid. The story told by the black activist Ms. Ivy Gcina concerned her experiences in prison, where she was brutally treated during interrogation. Tutu pulled some pages from his pocket and, standing, he read the words of Ivy Gcina.

> The same night I saw a light at night and my cell was opened. I did not see who was opening my cell. I did not look at the person. She said to me, "Ivy, it is me. I have fetched your medicine." She rubbed me. She made me take my medicine. I told her that I could not even hold anything but I can try. I told her I was going to try by all means. She said "It is fine, do not worry yourself. I will help you." So she made me take the medicine and then she massaged me. Then after that I could at least try and sleep.

This story had been told to the Truth and Reconciliation Commission chaired by Tutu. "A few days later," Tutu went on to add, "the local newspaper, the *Eastern Province Herald*, carried a large front-page picture of Ivy Gcina hugging Irene Crouse, accompanied by the following report," which Tutu read to us:

> Tortured activist Ivy Gcina was yesterday reunited with her Angel of Mercy — the kind jailer who held her hand and tended her wounds after hours of brutal interrogation by security police. "I never thought you'd remember me," said Irene, 37, as the two women threw their arms around each other on the stoop, crying and laughing at the same time. Ivy, 59, replied: "but

after I was assaulted it was you who was there to help me, who entered my cell at night. Can you ever forget someone like that?"

"We met as human beings, as women," Ivy recalled. "There was such communication there. Ensuring I had a clean towel, asking me how I was. The relationship was so good." Irene felt she was "only doing her duty" when she helped Ivy.

Adolfo leaned forward and said, "When these very crises occur, very profound crises, there is growth. People experience these crises only to gain a new mentality with a new sense of life and not of death. We have to believe in human beings and try everything possible to recuperate the social body and regain balance with the planet and cosmos, right? The relation of man, the relation of women, relationships with God, with life; Saint Francis reminds us of the importance of the health and blessing of our brother the sun, our sister the moon, our sister the water, and our brother-wolf as we return to respecting ourselves for eternity."

I felt that the door had opened for an essential component of the conversation to be introduced, one we had touched on in other sessions but needed more time and space: the place of spirituality in social action and peacemaking. All of those gathered possessed a spiritual outlook of some kind, from Christianity in the cases of Desmond Tutu, Adolfo Pérez Esquivel, Máiread Corrigan Maguire, to Buddhism for the Dalai Lama and Aung San Suu Kyi, to Islam for Ebadi and indigenous spirituality for Rigoberta Menchú Tum. Often, in their writings, interviews and speeches, I had appreciated the candor they showed concerning the significant place of non-dogmatic spirituality in their personal lives and work.

The Inspiring Spirit of Social Action

I opened the conversation briefly by saying, "I would like to turn our attention to the place of spirituality in your lives and work. How do you think about spirituality today and especially its role in relation to the resolution of conflict?"

Adolfo answered, "We have to respect the spirituality of the people, which is more and more in crisis. There is an incessant search with little sense of transcendence and we are spiritual beings and in this moment there is a sort of spiritual vacuum. The reestablishment of this harmony between transcendence and humanity's immanence is necessary. I think much of its value has been lost." To this Aung San Suu Kyi added, "The spiritual dimension becomes particularly important in a struggle in which deeply held convictions and strength of mind are the chief weapons against armed repression."

"I think that we all need to be healed," Máiread began, "and that's why we need ourselves to take time to be quiet, time to meditate, and time to rid ourselves of the anger and frustration in all the war that's going on within our own hearts. Peace starts within our own hearts."

The Dalai Lama nodded in agreement and added, "Peace starts within each one of us. When we have inner peace, we can be at peace with those around us. These days we human beings are very much involved in the external world, while we neglect the internal world. We do need scientific development and material development in order to survive and to increase the general benefit and prosperity, but equally as much we need mental peace. Yet no doctor can give you an injection of mental peace, and no market can sell it to you. If you go to a supermarket with millions and millions of dollars, you can buy anything, but if you go there and ask for peace of mind, people will laugh. And if you ask a doctor for genuine peace of mind, not the mere sedation you get from taking some kind of pill or injection, the doctor cannot help you. Even today's sophisticated computers cannot provide you with mental peace. Mental peace must come from the mind.

"Everyone wants happiness and pleasure, but if we compare physical pleasure and physical pain with mental pleasure and mental pain, we find that the mind is more effective, predominant, and superior. Thus it is worthwhile adopting certain methods to increase mental peace, and in order to do that it is important to know more about the mind. When we talk about preservation of the environment, it is related to many other things. Ultimately the decision must come from the human heart. The key point is to have a genuine sense of universal responsibility, based on love and compassion, and clear awareness," concluded the Dalai Lama.

Aung San Suu Kyi deepened the theme by relating it to contemplative practice. During her long periods of house arrest, I knew that she had developed a regular meditation practice, and it was about this that she began to speak.

"Not long before my house arrest in 1989," started Aung San Suu Kyi, "I was granted audience with the venerable U Pandita, an exceptional teacher in the best tradition of great spiritual mentors whose words act constantly as an aid to a better existence. *Hsayadaw* (holy teacher) U Pandita spoke of the importance of *samma-vaca* or right speech. Not only should one speak only the truth, one's speech should lead to harmony among beings, it should be kind and pleasant and it should be beneficial. One should follow the example of the Lord Buddha who only spoke words that were truthful and beneficial even if at times such speech was not always pleasing to the listener.

"The *Hsayadaw* also urged me to cultivate *sati*, mindfulness. Of the five spiritual faculties, *saddha* (faith), *viriya* (energy), *samadhi* (concentration), and *panna* (wisdom), it is only mindfulness that can never be in excess. Excessive faith without sufficient wisdom leads to blind faith, while excessive wisdom without sufficient faith leads to undesirable cunning. Too much energy combined with weak concentration leads to restlessness while strong concentration without sufficient energy leads to indolence. But as for mindfulness, one can never have too much of it, it is 'never in excess, but always in deficiency.' The truth and value of this Buddhist concept that *Hsayadaw* U Pandita took such pains to impress on me became evident during my years of house arrest.

"Like many Buddhist colleagues, I decided to put my time under detention to good use by practicing meditation. It was not an easy process. I did not have a teacher and my early attempts were more than a little frustrating. There were days when I found my failure to discipline my mind in accordance with prescribed meditation practices so infuriating I felt I was doing myself more harm than good. I think I would have given up but for the advice of a famous Buddhist teacher, that whether or not one wanted to practice meditation, one should do so for one's own good. So I gritted my teeth and kept at it, often rather glumly. Then my husband gave me a copy of *Hsayadaw* U Pandita's book, *In This Very Life: The Liberation Teachings of the Buddha*. By studying this book carefully, I learnt how to overcome the difficulties of meditation and to realize its benefits.

Aung San Suu Kyi

"In my political work I have been helped and strengthened by the teachings of members of the *sangha*. During my very first campaign trip across Burma, I received invaluable advice from monks in different parts of the country. In a monastery at Pakokku, the advice that an abbot gave to my father when he came to that town more than 40 years ago was repeated to me: 'Do not be frightened every time there is an attempt to frighten you, but do not be entirely without fear. Do not become elated every time you are praised, but do not be entirely lacking in elation.' In other words, while maintaining courage and humility, one should not abandon caution and healthy self-respect.

"Of the words of wisdom I gathered during that journey across central Burma, those of a 91-year-old *Hsayadaw* of Sagaing are particularly memorable. He sketched out for me tersely how it would be to work for democracy in Burma. 'You will be attacked and reviled for engaging in honest politics,' pronounced the *Hsayadaw* 'but you must persevere. Lay down an investment in *dukkha* [suffering] and you will gain *sukha* [bliss].'"

We all felt the weight of these last words. Aung San Suu Kyi, and many of those in our circle, had laid down a heavy investment in suffering. Bliss seemed remote for Burma, but we comforted ourselves with the accomplishments that had been achieved. Desmond Tutu beamed, and reminded us of the good that had been achieved.

"There is a lot of evil, there's no question about it, but there is also a lot of good," Tutu said. "And remember the riches that have been won. You know, there was slavery — of course, there's a modern version of it, but slavery was ended. There was Nazism — it looked like it was going to rule the roost, but it's beaten to dust. There was fascism; Spain, Portugal, and even the home of democracy, Greece, had a military dictatorship. And it's only been defeated in very recent years. And of course we overcame apartheid, even though there was a time when you thought, 'Oh, these guys are going to be there virtually forever.'

• • •

"What I am saying is that we shouldn't become despondent," Tutu went on. "We shouldn't want to give up. God doesn't give up on any of us, even on those we regard as the worst. This is part of the story for instance of Saul, who is a persecutor, turning to become Paul. There is nobody who is not transfigurable."

"On one of my first trips to Ecuador, I had a dream," said Adolfo, quietly. "I dreamt I saw Christ on the cross dressed in a poncho. Later I went to Riobamba, and happened to be visiting a community of the Litter Brothers of Jesus founded by Charles de Foucauld. I went into the chapel and there he was on the wall again — Christ crucified, in a poncho, as I had seen him in my dream. The image wasn't exactly the same, but it was Christ in a poncho. This struck me very much, and from then on he never let me alone.

"As an artist I have practically no time right now to do any work at all. But after I was released from La Plata Prison, I set myself to do a painting of *Christ in a Poncho*.

"He is the Christ of the poor. And he is a Christ without a face or hands or feet, for his face, hands, and feet are the faces, hands, and feet of the Indians and peasants of Latin America. Christ in a poncho is the presence of Christ in the poor."

I don't think that I was the only one who remembered Mother Teresa's justly famous response to the question, "What do you see in the faces of the poor and dying when you are caring for them?" Her reply was, "I see the face of Jesus." In other words, like Adolfo she saw the divine in its most sublime form in every human being.

Spirit and the Earth

Rigoberta Menchú Tum leaned forward and spoke in a lively manner directly from the heart about humanity and the Earth, about a spirituality that cared for all existence.

• • •

"The hope of the future that I see are the signals given to us by Mother Nature. There are earthquakes. There are hurricanes. There is suffering. But through all this we can reflect, we can think it over. My hope for the future is our capacity as human beings to humble ourselves before life, before the ages and times. That is my hope — that people return to thinking about life, return to thinking about the future, and once again consider their surroundings. I think there is hope there.

"Another great struggle is to avoid extremes, but rather to maintain a balance. There is no ideal world without it being in balance. So, radicalism — be it religious, political, spiritual — is negative for humanity. This is an equilibrium that can commence with our attitudes, but also take root in society. More equity, more equality can come through our leadership. Sometimes there are leaders who criticize me and say — 'How can you sit next to Chirac, and then sit next to a person from one of the more oppressed groups of the French people?' And I say, being with one side and then with the other is my obligation. I must be able to find a balanced point of view to be able to contribute. The balance helps us find positive propositions, viable propositions — if they aren't viable then we aren't contributing to build something better than what we have.

"I would like to be part of the millenary Mayan culture experience, not only in my life, but in the lives of others. I would like to be a light of Mayan spirituality. I want to have that great contact with my ancestors, and to have inherited something, these positive energies of reflection, of meditation . . . healing techniques, including healing of one's insides, when one is mentally sick or because of everything that happens around us.

"How can we confront the world and make it viable for others? The world of consumerism, of drug addiction, of alcoholism, and all the other vices . . . What can we do to save, one, two, ten, twenty of these souls that struggle with these vices? Then, also to look at life holistically I need to get deeper into the Mayan culture, and do everything possible in that sense: Mayan university, Mayan television . . . I don't know what things can be done.

Write many, many books; talk about the spirits of our ancestors, getting this vision through to the coming generations."

The words of her sister touched Wangari Maathai, who confessed, "I don't really know why I care so much. I just have something inside me that tells me that there is a problem, and I have got to do something about it. I think that is what I would call the God in me.

"All of us have a God in us, and that God is the spirit that unites all life, everything that is on this planet. It must be this voice that is telling me to do something, and I am sure it's the same voice that is speaking to everybody on this planet — at least everybody who seems to be concerned about the fate of the world."

Archbishop Desmond Tutu

18

A Final Word Concerning Love and Forgiveness

Our final session was about to begin. I wanted to lead the conversation to the theme of forgiveness, a topic on which Desmond Tutu had written and spoken extensively, and about which I expected others would have something to add. So, after everyone was seated once again, I asked, "All of you know the pain of oppression and persecution. You have suffered it yourself and have witnessed it in many others. In your opinions, in a post-conflict region, what is the right balance between justice and forgiveness?"

Of Justice and Forgiveness

Shirin Ebadi, who had practiced law and was Iran's first woman judge, responded first. "I believe when an individual, people or society is under oppression, revenge is the worst solution. And at the same time, forgetting the past is not a good solution either because it allows the traumatic experiences of the past to happen again. Indeed, we must forgive past errors and oppressions that have been done unto us, but not forget them."

In Jody Williams's remarks that followed, the tension between justice and forgiveness was palpable. "I think it's complicated. Should you just have a great opening of emotions and discussing the problems, or do those who have really violated humanity also have to be brought to justice? What's the balance? I think that you have to have some sort of forgiveness and reconciliation for any society that has suffered huge trauma to move forward. But I also think that those who have acted with grotesque impunity have to be brought to justice. I do believe in that kind of justice."

Desmond Tutu entered quite naturally, putting forward his considered reflections of the issue. "I think that if people have been discriminated against," he began, "and if they have been hurt and even traumatized — if we don't do anything about it, there are going to be repercussions. What I think of is the kind of trauma where there's no social healing in places like Northern Ireland or the Middle East. In South Africa, they are trying to heal the hurts of the past to help the community, to help society make up for the horrors of the past. Helping people become whole again, help people maybe move from feeling resentment and anger and perhaps longing for revenge — moving towards the possibilities of forgiveness, of reconciliation, of wholeness.

"In forgiving, people are not being asked to forget," Tutu went on. "On the contrary, it is important to remember, so that we should not let such atrocities happen again. Forgiveness does not mean condoning what has been done. It means taking what happened seriously and not minimizing it; drawing out the sting in the memory that threatens to poison our existence. It involves trying to understand the perpetrators and to have empathy, to try to stand in their shoes and appreciate the sort of pressures and influences that might have conditioned them. Forgiveness is not being sentimental."

Tutu attempted to make his point clearer. "I have used the following analogy to try to explain the need for a perpetrator to confess. Imagine you are sitting in a dank, stuffy, dark room. This is because the curtains are drawn and the windows have been shut. Outside the light is shining and a fresh breeze is blowing. If you want the light to stream into that room and the fresh air to flow in, you will have to open the window and draw the curtains apart; then that light which has always been available will come in and air will enter the room to freshen it up. So it is with forgiveness. The victim may be ready to forgive and make the gift of her forgiveness available, but it is up to the wrongdoer to appropriate the gift—to open the window and draw the curtains aside. He does this by acknowledging the wrong he had done, so letting the light and fresh air of forgiveness enter his being."

Tutu paused for a moment and then went on. "In the act of forgiveness we are declaring our faith in the future of a relationship and in the capacity of the wrongdoer to make a new beginning on a course that will be different from the one that caused us the wrong. We are saying here is a chance to make a new beginning. It is an act of faith that the wrongdoer can change. According to Jesus, we should be ready to do this not just once, not just seven times, but 70 times seven, without limit—provided, it seems Jesus says, your brother or sister who has wronged you is ready to come and confess the wrong they have committed yet again.

"That is difficult, but because we are not infallible, because we will hurt especially the ones we love by some wrong, we will always need a process of forgiveness and reconciliation to deal with those unfortunate yet all too human breaches in relationships. They are an inescapable characteristic of the human condition.

"Once the wrongdoer has confessed and the victim has forgiven, it does not mean that is the end of the process. Most frequently, the wrong has affected the victim in tangible, material ways. Apartheid provided the whites with enormous benefits and privileges, leaving its victims deprived and exploited. If someone steals my pen and then asks me to forgive him, unless he returns my pen the sincerity of his contrition and confession will be considered to be nil. Confession, forgiveness, and reparation, wherever feasible, form part of a continuum."

The persecution of the Tibetan people by the Chinese, especially the bru-tality shown towards Buddhist monks, had deeply affected the Dalai Lama, and yet he seemed capable of setting these actions aside, forgiving them and seeking ways to establish better relationships with the Chinese. I asked him, how did he think of forgiveness?

"In my own case, in Tibet, all this destruction, death, all happened, such painful experiences. But revenge . . . this creates unhappiness. So, think with a wider perspective: revenge is not good, so forgive. Forgiveness does not mean you forget about the past. We should be aware that these past sufferings happened because of narrow-mindedness on both sides. So now, time has passed. We feel more wise, more developed. I think that's the only way."

"How do you foster forgiveness?" I asked.

"First, according to my own experience, I think of others, including my so-called enemies. These people are also human beings. They also have the same right to achieve happiness and avoid suffering. Then second — my future is related with them; my interest is related with their interest. For example: my country, my people are very much related with the Chinese. Our future very much depends on them. Taking care of them is ultimately taking care of ourselves.

"I often tell people about one of my friends," continued the Dalai Lama, "one old monk, he spent many years, almost two decades, in the Chinese Gulag. After he came to India, he told me that after almost two decades in a Chinese Gulag, on a few occasions he felt he was in danger. And I asked, 'What kind of danger?' And his answer was, 'Danger of losing com-passion towards the Chinese.' So he considered the development of nega-tive feeling, ill feeling towards others to be the most destructive. He feels losing compassion is very dangerous, very serious. So as a result, Buddhism was a tremendous help to keep his own mind more calm. And that, I think, is very, very helpful in facing the difficulties of life."

"It is important to acknowledge that we have all been hurt over the years," Máiread added, "that we have hurt each other. More than anything, we are in need of forgiveness. I believe this is a key to building a genuine reconciled and healed community. Forgiveness does not come easy. It is a long, hard process. People are not being asked to forget the past, but rather to make a choice to forgive and move forward into a new future.

"Forgiveness is the only way to personal peace. Even after 'justice' has been done, many families have felt they needed something 'more.' Then they themselves chose to forgive and let go of resentment. They released themselves from the need for punishment and revenge. Without forgiveness, there can be no real healing of ourselves, each other, or our community. Revenge keeps the violence circulating. Together with pride, the desire for revenge hardens our hearts against forgiveness. Punishment does not bring the victim inner peace of mind. Only the victim choosing to forgive can do that. Even after an offender has served a lifetime in prison, the victims often do not feel inner peace until they themselves make the decision to forgive."

Of Love

"Forgiveness," I responded, "appears to me to be deeply related to love. What is the place of love in these considerations?" Betty Williams gave a passionate and immediate response to my question.

"There are all different kinds of love," Betty began, "and there's a very, very, very thin line between love and hate. It can flip in an absolute second, and power does that. Power converts love to hate if it's not used correctly. And that's what we see now. I just don't understand how power can turn love so quickly to hate . . . but love's all-consuming to me, it really is."

Betty paused and continued at a slower and more measured pace. "But compassion is more important than intellect in calling forth the love that the work of peace needs, and intuition can often be a far more powerful

Jody Williams and Rigoberta Menchú Tum

searchlight than cold reason. We have to think, and think hard, but if we do not have compassion before we even start thinking, then we are quite likely to start fighting over theories . . .

"Because of the role of women over so many centuries in so many different cultures, they have been excluded from what have been called public affairs; for that very reason they have concentrated much more on things close to home . . . and they have kept far more in touch with the true realities . . . the realities of giving birth and love. The moment has perhaps come in human history when, for very survival, those realities must be given pride of place over the vainglorious adventures that lead to war.

"The only force which can break down those barriers is the force of love, the force of trust, soul-force . . . . We are deeply, passionately dedicated to the cause of nonviolence, to the force of truth and love, to soul-force. To those who say that we are naïve, utopian idealists, we say that we are the only realists, and that those who continue to support militarism in our time are supporting the progress towards total self-destruction of the human race, when the only right and left will be dead to the right and dead to the left, and death and destruction right, left and center, east and west, north and south."

Although we could have taken the topic of love much further, the day was getting late and I was anxious to ask one or two more questions. The first was to inquire about what they might achieve by working together. "Each of you works incredibly hard for the causes closest to your heart: human rights, environment, and so on. Have you considered the possibility of working more closely together from time to time, and if so what might you undertake?"

To this the Dalai Lama replied, "One thing — ever since the Iraq crisis happened, I have very strongly felt that those individuals who represent no one — no country — but can be a representative of peace, a representative of humanity, including many Nobel Laureates; they should take a more active role for peace. And therefore, whenever some crisis is about to rise up, about to come, I urgently appeal to Nobel Laureates in such cases that we should come as a group, go there and talk to the key people.

"I feel that before the Iraq crisis, if some Nobel Laureates went to Baghdad and gave Saddam Hussein very frankly all the possibilities and consequences, I think that he as a human being and from his own selfish viewpoint, of course, he'd have to think. Even if the mission failed, nothing would be lost. This is my appeal. I wrote about this idea to President Havel and also Nelson Mandela and some others, and eventually I also personally met with them and discussed this, and Nelson Mandela was very, very supportive and President Havel was very supportive. So, I am hopeful. I am looking forward to some active role by those Nobel Peace Laureates in PeaceJam."

Rigoberta answered by saying, "The grandeur of the Nobel Peace Prize is not really the prize but rather the incalculable work that each one of the Nobel winners does. It is the message of peace that we try to build every day. It is the effort of many people who believe in us and fight with us. And because of this I believe is it very important to say that the Nobel Peace Prize is a sign of hope, that it is a tiny light inside all of the efforts and energies of a world that fights and battles every day.

"What are we going to do? I think we must renew our commitment so that the fight for justice is a life-long fight; the fight against impunity is a life-long fight; that the fight for peace is something so vital so as to actually renew the contents of peace. And I think that we are the hope of a culture of peace. This culture that has to be born out of tolerance, of dialogue, of non-discrimination, and of inclusion. This peaceful culture does not only accept difficulties but looks for solutions. I think that we are people who try to look for solutions every day.

"I think all of the friends of the Nobel Peace Prize winners have invaluable experience. Above all, what can we do so that PeaceJam continues to be a light for youth and continues to inspire them? I hope that PeaceJam not only celebrates these ten years but also is able to celebrate all of the coming years with the help of all of the Nobel Prize winners, including future Nobel laureates. I hope that the youth who are in PeaceJam will also be a source of hope and develop successful work for a better world."

Shirin Ebadi added her vision. "The Nobel Peace Prize winners are now living in many different parts of the world: Asia, Africa, Europe, America, and South America. Keeping in mind that women everywhere are facing problems and Nobel Laureates are very familiar with the problems of women in their respective countries, they can join hands in order to help solve these problems. If we combine our efforts we can become much stronger."

Oscar Arias spoke of his great hopes for a different future. "I would want, in an ideal world, to have societies in which no one lacks the necessities. That we are able to satisfy the most elementary needs of human beings; a more just world, more united, more tolerant, with greater respect for diversity. A world in which there is compassion, love, and justice; a world in which we are able to say with great joy that we defeated poverty, and that poverty is no more than a sad memory of past generations. This requires redefining values, redefining priorities; to begin to generate in the minds of the younger generations a new ethics and this is all of our responsibility."

As each member of the circle spoke about their hopes and intentions, the whole group pulled a little closer together, recognizing that although much had been accomplished, much more still remained to be done. The Dalai Lama affirmed the importance of the will to act, saying, "The prime mover of every human action is the motivation or the determination. Firstly, our motivation should be simple and sincere. Whether we achieve the goal or not does not matter so long as our motivation is very sincere and we make an attempt. Finally, even if we fail to achieve our goal we won't regret making the effort. If our motivation is not sincere, even if the objective is achieved the person will not be so happy or satisfied deep down. So motivation is very important." All present possessed the pure motivation about which he was speaking. The Dalai Lama's remarks reminded Máiread of the wise words of the Christian monastic Thomas Merton.

"This question reminded me of Thomas Merton's advice to peacemakers," Máiread began, "when he cautioned them not to make the mistake of becoming 'success oriented' and fail to recognize that the diseases we struggle against might be too complex and too far advanced for us. He felt that insisting on evidence of success might quickly lead us to despair and paralysis." If little is achieved in one's lifetime, the many friends made along the way and the love of the deed itself, these are their own reward. The quality of our human relationships possesses a saving power, which is another way to say that the love between us is what will save everything.

Absent but not Forgotten

As Máiread finished speaking, footsteps could be heard in the hall and a somber military figure moved into the doorway. The time for Aung San Suu Kyi's departure had come. With few words, she moved from one friend to the next wishing each well, giving each a hand and warm smile. I overheard Rigoberta say, "And, Aung San Suu Kyi, as a Maya, I want to wish you much spirituality, much concentration, much confidence because the Creator strengthens us every time we are looking for energy."

With grace and equanimity she walked to the door, turned and bowed in a sign of respect to us all. The room was full of unspoken words of encouragement, and also righteous anger. Aung San Suu Kyi had spoken so beautifully about what mattered most. We all sensed that her delicate physique held a great soul, one that radiated wisdom to the entire world from her house and prison in Burma.

After she had departed, Rigoberta Menchú Tum unleashed the first torrent. "Well, the situation of Aung San Suu Kyi represents a shame that humanity should feel. It can't be possible for a Nobel Peace Prize Winner to be a prisoner without rights. It can't be possible to quiet a person who represents a whole population and that these people are equally silenced. I think solidarity has to be more effective. So I wish much success to Aung San Suu Kyi. We are very sorry because it is part of our shame. I hope that more people feel ashamed for the deprivation of the rights and liberties that Aung San Suu Kyi has lived through for many years now. May Aung San Suu Kyi live in the hearts of humanity!"

Shirin Ebadi joined in a heartfelt expression of regret. "I am very sorry about what has happened to Ms. Aung San Suu Kyi. I am very sorry and very surprised that a government can be so indifferent to worldwide opinion in this regard. I think for as long as this government is behaving this way, other countries that believe in democracy and respect human rights should not have diplomatic relations or trade relations with this country. I am very sorry that a lady who has won the Nobel Peace Prize and all of her struggles for peace are through nonviolent methods, is now for years under house arrest and the world only expresses its sadness in this regard, and more interestingly the Burmese government does not heed any of the international outcry and is not willing to change its wrongful course of action. This is clearly in violation of human rights and the Human Rights Assembly must seriously address the wrongful actions of the Burmese government."

Wangari Maathai spoke for everyone when she said, "All of us in the family of the Nobel Peace Prize Laureates continue to be very concerned about our sister and fellow Laureate who continues to be under arrest. We continue to hope that this new consciousness that we're talking about gets to more and more people, especially in decision-making circles. That people, our leaders especially, will realize that the time has come for us to respect each other's freedoms, to respect our human rights, to give each other space, to allow for diversity of opinions. Because we are diverse we must learn to tolerate diverse opinions and to give each other space — democratic space, where we can be listened to whether we are powerful or weak, whether we are many or few, whether we are rich or poor. I know that our sister is working to create space for a great many people. I hope that sooner than later, that cloud will rise and we shall see her in freedom."

Betty was furious. "I know all of the Laureates are extremely angry about the situation Suu's in. She's done enough suffering. It's time to release Aung San Suu Kyi, and we'd all love to be there. As the Dalai Lama said once today, the day that we get her out, I'd love for all the Laureates to be there to greet her with a big hug, because all of us remember her every day in our prayers. There's not a day goes by that I don't think of Suu, and how she's withstood that enormous — I mean, this tiny little woman is keeping the whole SLORC regime at bay, and she's using the techniques of nonviolence. What an example. I couldn't demonstrate this. I don't have that kind of courage. She's so courageous, she really is."

As Betty finished, everyone began speaking at once. Suu's chair was empty, but she was not forgotten. Plans were afoot for a campaign by which all

Aung San Suu Kyi remains under house arrest behind these steel gates today.

the Laureates would participate on Daw Suu's behalf, reaffirming their solidarity with the people of Burma and their legitimate struggle for democracy, human rights and civilian rule. Tyranny does not crumble by itself. Freedom must be demanded and defended, by those who have been denied it and by those who are already free.

It was a miracle to have had her with us, something only possible in our most loving fantasy. But now that she was gone I could feel the circle of Nobels was being called back from three days of retreat to a world that needed them, as it also needs all of us, to act.

Bibliography

In writing this book I have drawn heavily on PeaceJam's One Voice Dialogue interview series, and PeaceJam's own archive of interviews and speeches by the Nobel Laureates. In addition I have made use of the following sources.

Adolfo Pérez Esquivel
> Adolfo Pérez Esquivel, *Christ in a Poncho: Witnesses to the Nonviolent Struggles in Latin America* (Maryknoll, NY: Orbis Books, 1983).

Aung San Suu Kyi
> Aung San Suu Kyi, *Freedom from Fear*, Revised edition (London: Penguin, 1995).
> Aung San Suu Kyi, *Letters from Burma*, introduction by Fergal Keane (London: Penguin, 1997).

The Dalai Lama
> Tenzin Gyatso, the Dalai Lama, *Freedom in Exile* (New York: HarperCollins, 1990).
> Tenzin Gyatso, the Dalai Lama, *Ethics for the New Millennium* (New York, Riverhead Books, 1999).
> The Dalai Lama and Victor Chan, *The Wisdom of Forgiveness* (New York: Riverhead Books, 2004).

Desmond Tutu
> Desmond Tutu, *The Rainbow People of God: The Making of a Peaceful Revolution* (New York: Doubleday, 1994).
> Desmond Tutu, *No Future Without Forgiveness* (New York: Doubleday, 1999).
> Desmond Tutu, *God Has a Dream: A Vision of Hope for Our Time* (New York: Doubleday, 2004).

Jody Williams
> Shawn Roberts and Jody Williams, *After the Guns Fall Silent: The Enduring Legacy of Landmines* (Washington, D.C.: Vietnam Veterans of America Foundation, 1995).

José Ramos-Horta

José Ramos-Horta, *Funu: The Unfinished Saga of East Timor* (Trenton, NJ: Red Sea Press, 1987).

Joseph Rotblat

Robert Hinde and Joseph Rotblat, *War No More: Eliminating Conflict in the Nuclear Age* (London: Pluto Press, 2003).

Máiread Corrigan Maguire

Máiread Corrigan Maguire, *The Vision of Peace: Faith and Hope in Northern Ireland* (Maryknoll, NY: Orbis, 1999).

Máiread Corrigan and Betty Williams

Sarah Buscher and Bettina Ling, *Máiread Corrigan and Betty Williams: Making Peace in Northern Ireland* (New York: Feminist Press at The City University of New York, 1999).

Rigoberta Menchú

Elisabeth Burgos-Debray, ed. *I, Rigoberta Menchu: An Indian Woman in Guatemala*, translated by Ann Wright (London: Verso, 1984).

Shirin Ebadi

Shirin Ebadi, with Azadeh Moaveni, *Iran Awakening: A Memoir of Revolution and Hope* (New York: Random House, 2006).

Wangari Maathai

Wangari Maathai, "Speak Truth to Power," an essay in the book *Speak Truth to Power*, edited by Kerry Kennedy (New York: Umbrage, 2004).

On PeaceJam

Darcy Gifford, *PeaceJam: How Young People Can Make Peace in their Schools and Communities* (San Francisco: Jossey-Bass, 2004).

Copyrights reserved, used with permission.

We would like to acknowledge the generous support
of the Fetzer Institute for the One Voice Dialogue project
and the insightful guidance of Tom Callanan, which
made this global conversation between
twelve leading Nobel Peace Laureates possible.

PeaceJam's two founders, Dawn Gifford Engle and Ivan Suvanjieff,
brought enthusiasm and skill to the design and execution
of the One Voice Dialogue project, which were the preconditions
for this book. In a matter of months they traveled the globe in order
to repeatedly interview the Nobel Laureates featured here:
an extraordinary effort and accomplishment.
We would also like to acknowledge the tireless and capable work
of editorial assistant Gary L. Blackwell, Jr., and the gifted design team
at Impress, Inc. led by Hans Teensma.
Finally, we sincerely thank the Nobel Laureates and their staffs
for their time and attention to this project, without which
this book would have been impossible.